The Interpretation of Dreams and Nightmares

The Interpretation of Dreams and Nightmares

SANDRA SHULMAN

CASTLE BOOKS

This book was originally published in England by Macdonald Unit 75 under the title *Dreams*. It is here reprinted by arrangement.

Contents

Introduction

SINCE the birth of mankind dreaming has been a never-ending source of wonder, inspiration, and terror. It is one of those involuntary experiences, which affects every human being from primitive tribesman to urbanised office-worker, and links each of us to all the people who have ever lived ... irrespective of century or continent.

Obviously what we do know of our ancestors' dreams has come down to us from written records. Yet, we can be equally certain that their unlettered predecessors also dreamed simply because they possessed mental faculties similar to our own. We are able to test this theory in those outposts of our world where the people are still at the primitive stage of evolution. They may not even be aware of the existence of other tribes let alone able to read or write, but according to anthropologists they do dream ...

Sometimes a dream is so delightful you hope to dream it all over again, or if woken in the middle you try to go back to sleep to recapture that wonderful other world. But dreams can also be horrific, containing your particular terrors, so that afterwards you dread to shut your eyes in case you sleep and repeat those events.

Thus, besides being universal, dreaming is also a very subjective business, characterised by our deepest selves, and experienced in the total solitude of our own sleep. You may be able to relate your dream next day, but the happening took place for you alone ... as if you were the audience-of-one and main participant in a drama which seemed to be of your own creation, because it is part of you, yet beyond your control ...

For the majority of people the process of dreaming can be described as an extraordinary kaleidoscope of visual images which visit us during sleep yet involve emotion and senses. We seem to hear sounds, smell pleasant or unpleasant odours, actually laugh, weep, talk, sweat, and walk because of the contents of our dreams, which are frequently – by waking standards – devoid of logic, although at the time they might appear to be making perfect sense.

If we are able to recall these shifting fantasies on waking most of us will admit to being intrigued or perturbed ... even if we belong to that rather pragmatic school of thought which tends to dismiss their sole cause as late-night cheese-eating. Again and again the individual asks: do my dreams mean something ... or nothing? Why do I dream?

Across the centuries countless attempts have been made to answer these questions, and solve the secret of dreams in terms of particular cultural beliefs. Though often naïve, and sometimes completely unintelligible to modern minds, the explanations of dream symbols offered by ancient religion and magic were the fore-runners of the sophisticated interpretations employed in 20th-century psychoanalysis.

It is impossible to introduce the subject of dreams without some discussion of symbolism . . . that a person, object, creature, or situation can represent an abstract concept or some actuality to which it doesn't relate at first sight. The cross of Christianity is a simple device, yet it synthesises a vast area of worldwide faith, history, and thought, and no one would mistake the object for the religion. People rally to a banner, not because it is a brightly-coloured pennant, but because it symbolises a homeland or a cause. The bluebird is a real bird, but in many minds it is associated with the elusive emotion, happiness.

The meaning behind any particular symbol need not of course be general, which further complicates dream interpretation. We would have to know a lot more about a dreamer before we could say a dream containing a cross had something to do with religion. If he were not a Christian, then the symbol would not necessarily have a religious significance. It might represent some cross-roads situation in waking life . . . or even be a verbal pun about being cross with some person or event.

You may have dreamed of being lost in a dense forest. If you have a very down-to-earth mind you might well insist that such a dream simply means what it depicts. The dream may mean nothing more than that, perhaps springing from some memory of an actual experience. There again the trees might *symbolise* problems among which in waking life you seem to wander unable to find a way out. After all, we do have that useful phrase which represents a similar situation: 'I couldn't see the wood for the trees . . .'

The quantity of dream books sold today show how many of us consult their sometimes widely differing interpretations, which also means we are accepting in some part the idea of symbols. Probably we find the arbitrary answers rather unsatisfactory, yet from such books emerges an important fact about dreams: that though diverse experiences, memories, and conditionings separate individual sleepers they do frequently share similar dream symbols. Because of this, interpreters have always been able to categorise dreams . . . however roughly.

Just discuss the subject with a group of friends. You'll be surprised at the similarities which occur . . . dreams of flying, falling, death, nudity, losing teeth, or missing trains.

These dream books sold on station bookstalls are the mass-produced descendants of writings consulted by our remotest ancestors. Clay tablets found at Ninevah, that belonged to the library of the Assyrian King Ashurbanipal, who reigned six centuries before Christ, contain material dating back to 5000 BC, and show that the Assyrians shared our curiosity about dreaming.

They employed banishing rituals to drive out the effects of demons who caused bad dreams, and believed that the interpretation of unpleasant dreams helped discover the reason for, and also cure, a dreamer's affliction.

Thousands of years and a host of technological achievements may divide us from the ancient inhabitants of Mesopotamia, but interpretations in today's popular dream books are often similar to those accepted by the Assyrians.

They believed that someone who dreamed of flying frequently, not far above the ground, would lose his possessions, and a modern interpretation warns that flying too low in your dreams heralds disaster. If an Assyrian dreamed about a bird then he would regain a lost possession. For some modern interpreters the same dream predicts unexpected good luck. Dreams of urination, according to the Assyrian Book of Dreams, symbolise virility and procreative activities. Later in this book we shall see that Freud and his followers shared similar opinions.

Claims about the purposes of dreams have been many: to predict the future; to convey messages from the gods to men; to diagnose and cure sickness; to be a fountainhead of themes and a literary device for poets.

Eastern and Oriental cultures held that during sleep the soul left the body to indulge in wild adventures involving other people's souls, including those of the dead. They found it impossible to distinguish between fantasy and reality, so that whatever happened in a dream must have actually taken place . . . even if it was technically impossible, or utterly ludicrous.

Pockets of such belief exist today. Among certain African tribes to dream of committing adultery incurs the same punishment as the physical act. Some Red Indians treat people who dream of having been bitten by a snake as if they're literally suffering from snake bite. In fairly primitive regions it is still considered dangerous to waken a sleeper too suddenly: if the wandering soul hasn't had enough time to return to its body it might angrily attack the disturber of sleep . . .

Dreams might have remained in the nebulous atmosphere of poetry, superstition, and fairground quackery, but at the end of the last century a Viennese doctor, Sigmund Freud, saw them as the keys with which to unlock the door of man's unconscious. His famous book *The Interpretation of Dreams* started a revolution in the approach to the whole subject. Freud's theories marked the dividing point between the old and new attitude towards dreaming, but in its attempts to heal and understand the troubled mind psychoanalysis did not spurn to examine the ancient beliefs about the meanings and sources of dreams.

In our age, when the furthest star or minutest particle leads to complex probing and experiment, it is strange to realise that the dark continent of sleep, which accounts for a third of our life, has only comparatively recently become a territory to explore and chart. A good part of this apparently inactive area is now known to be devoted to dreams and science is beginning to raise the age-old subject out of the realms of superstition, and often brilliant hypothesis, into the unemotional light of the laboratory. Soon we may be on the brink of penetrating the really significant mysteries of the human unconscious – the only route by which we can ever hope to understand man himself . . .

I

Before Freud

THE language of dreams is pictorial, and the images presented are often symbols which dramatise and obscure the message, so that a dream cannot always be accepted on its face value. This is no modern discovery. From earliest times men realised that these symbols had to be translated into some kind of rational and intelligible form . . . and that this task required a specialised vocational talent, which was probably sometimes feigned or exaggerated to enhance and enrich reputations, pockets, and temples.

Oneirology – the study and interpretation of dreams – was originally associated with the inseparably entwined mystic roots of civilisation: religion and magic, the all-powerful secret provinces of kings, priests, and magicians. Medicine was closely allied to these mysteries: for healing was regarded as divine or magic, just as the source of much illness might be ascribed to demons or the wrath of a god. Both Imhotep and Aesculapius were mortal, and undoubtedly skilled doctors by the standards of their own times, before death elevated them to become the gods of healing in ancient Egypt and Greece respectively.

Most of us have some knowledge of how much influence oneirology had on the antique world from reading the Bible. Genesis gives an account of the young dreamer Joseph, who, able to interpret the symbols in his own dreams, predicted that one day he would become an important personage before whom his whole family would pay homage. 'Behold, I have dreamed a dream more; and, behold the sun and the moon and the eleven stars made obeisance before me . . .'

From this we get a clear example of ancient dream language: the sun, in this case, was Joseph's father, the moon not unnaturally his mother, and the eleven stars his eleven brothers. As we shall see, the meanings of symbols are not always universal: they spring from the deepest beliefs of a particular society, or the character of an individual relating to his environment, personal memories, and perhaps mankind's memories.

Not surprisingly, Joseph's interpretations increased his brothers' envy. Later, he left an Egyptian prison to become the second most powerful man in the kingdom through his interpretative powers, which having successfully explained fellow prisoners' dreams allowed him to solve the riddle of Pharoah's dreams after all the Egyptian magicians and wise men had failed.

The Book of Daniel gives a fair picture of how much credence Babylonians placed on oneirology. Though an alien captive, Daniel won great favour with King

Nebuchadnezzar for revealing the substance and meaning of certain royal dreams, which magicians, astrologers, sorcerers, and Chaldeans had been unable to do.

In the New Testament, the appearance of angels in dreams caused the flight and return of the Holy Family.

... behold, the angel of the Lord appeareth to Joseph in a dream, saying, Arise, and take the young child and his mother and flee into Egypt...

But when Herod was dead, behold, an angel of the Lord appeareth in a dream to Joseph in Egypt, Saying, Arise, and take the young child and his mother, and go into the land of Israel: for they are dead which sought the young child's life...

Such prophetic sleeping visions are seen as divinely inspired, and are the features of other great world faiths. Buddha's mother and father foresaw through dreams that their son would abandon worldly goods to become a wandering monk, and before his own enlightenment Buddha had five dreams foretelling the momentous event.

For Mahomet 'the dream is a conversation between man and his God', but Islam's attitude to oneirology was rigidly bound by its concern with orthodoxy in religious matters and the maintainance of a strict social order. Dreams were not to be discussed with women, whose own dreams could only be taken into account if the females were upright, chaste, and married. Interpreters had to be very devout Moslems, and dreams were regarded as 'true' or 'false'; the former were those in which the Prophet, angels, kings, teachers, or parents appeared, i.e. upholders of authority; the latter contained demons, heretical ideas, or were the products of self-interest.

Islam followed the Jewish tradition that suspected the 'dreamer of dreams' who might lead the faithful into error, although some Islamic religious customs, such as the muezzin's call to prayer, were instigated as a result of dreams.

We get a fascinating glimpse of what the creators of the pyramids thought about dreaming from the Chester Beatty Papyrus, housed in the British Museum. It came originally from Thebes in Upper Egypt, and although written around 1350 BC incorporates far older material. The Egyptian word for dream derives from the verb 'to awaken', which suggests a profound philosophy about the whole process. Interpretation was performed in the 'houses of life' by special priests – 'masters of secret things' – who were members of the religious and social hierarchy.

Just as subsequent civilisations borrowed from them, the Egyptians grafted Babylonian and Assyrian dream theories on to their own.

In interpreting certain dreams the Assyrians held opposites to be the truth. So, if you dreamed you were cursed by a god, your prayer would be accepted, but if your dream showed you were being blessed you'd better be prepared for the god's wrath. A dream of descending into hell foretold a long life. Similar converses are found among ancient Egyptian writings where to dream of death predicted a long life. These contrary interpretations are also a feature of modern dream books: death equals life, to be cursed foretells the successful realisation of an ambition.

Many of the recorded Egyptian dreams were divine messages sent by the gods to kings and priests, warning, predicting, or demanding certain deeds, which had to be obeyed. Ptolemy Soter dreamed of a huge statue which told him to return it to Alexandria – its original site. When he wakened, he ordered that the statue should be sought for. It was then found and replaced. An inscription before the sphinx at Giza describes how Thutmose IV, who reigned circa 1450 BC, dreamed that the god Hormakhu vowed him the kingdom. When he did become king Thutmose ordered the sands to be cleared away from the sphinx.

Ordinary dreams were categorised as 'good' or 'bad'. From this distance in time we cannot know the precise importance of particular objects, words, or acts in the world of ancient Egyptians, so some of their interpretations are bound to seem arbitrary and irrational.

The appearance of the moon in a dream signified a pardon, a snake meant provisions. If a woman dreamed of giving birth to a crocodile or a cat she would have many children, but if she kissed her husband in a dream she would have trouble! To catch a bird foretold the loss of possessions. It was 'good' to dream of cutting wood because it signified the destruction of enemies, but it was 'bad' to dream of falling teeth, which foretold the dreamer's own destruction.

Dreams of teeth have particular significance in all societies. Today's interpreters often explain falling, decayed, or stained teeth as a warning of future unhappiness.

A remote ancestor of modern psychotherapy was incubation – the sacred dream therapy practised in Assyria, Egypt, the Graeco-Roman civilisation, eastern religions, by early Christians and Moslems, among many primitive tribes, and still to be encountered in some parts of today's world. In Japan the sick sleep in temples dedicated to the 'master of healing' and claim that he visits them in their sleep in the guise of a monk. The induced dreams of Buddhism were supposed to lead to an awakening in the mind similar to that produced through psychoanalysis.

Afflicted people went to sacred temples, caves, grottos, groves or springs where special priests induced sleep with ritual, incantations, and probably drugs. During a dream the god would appear, and perhaps indicate a treatment for the illness. Originally, the priests merely recorded the dreamer's experience. Interpretation evolved with time. Healing depended more on the fact of a dream occurring rather than any subsequent medication. We might describe it as a form of faith-healing, based on the ardent wish of the dreamer to be cured, in surroundings specially 'sympathetic' to illness. As the majority of problems seemed to have been of a sexual nature incubation was often considered the cure for sterility.

Both the Greeks and Romans, as well as incorporating the theories of 'true' and 'false', divine and predictive dreams, placed particular emphasis on incubation. It was practised in over three hundred temples dedicated to Aesculapius ruled over by the priests of the oracle. The cures – and obviously records of those exist rather than failures – were probably not very different from the ones which sometimes occur at sacred centres of present-day religious pilgrimage such as Lourdes and Fatima. Often those distant illnesses must have been of a hysterical, psychosomatic, or self-induced origin, and the fact of having the priests' attention, performing a required sacrifice, and following a rigorous regime eradicated much of the trouble. Sometimes, of course, this dream therapy must have resulted in tragic circumstances for cases of acute mental anguish.

Hippocrates, called the father of medicine, who lived in the 4th century before Christ, wrote a treatise on dreams. From it we get some idea of how contemporary incubation worked.

Particular dream symbols were connected with states of health so that certain illnesses might be detected before any physical symptoms manifested themselves. To dream of the sun, moon, or stars in their normal conditions meant the dreamer was healthy. However, any deviation in a celestial body's behaviour indicated some sickness which required a specified treatment.

If the moon is involved, it is advisable to draw off the harmful matter internally; therefore use an emetic. . . . If the sun encounters any of these changes, the trouble is more violent and less easy to expel. The drawing-off should be produced both ways. . . . If the heavenly bodies are seen dimly in a clear sky, and shine weakly, and seemed to be stopped from revolving by dryness, then it is a sign there is a danger of incurring sickness. Exercise should be stopped ...

Heavenly bodies wandering off their proper courses signified some mental disturbance caused by anxiety. If a star moved upwards it meant fluxes in the head; movement towards the sea a disease of the bowels; movement eastwards tumours in the flesh ...

Modern eyebrows probably lift sceptically at such diagnoses. Yet many doctors consider certain dreams might have a physiological cause. A Viennese heart specialist of the 1930s suggested that dreams of nudity were triggered off by a disturbance in blood circulation. Havelock Ellis, who did a vast amount of research on dreaming at the end of the last century, considered that dreams were a product of mind and body. He cited an example of someone being woken by a dream about intruders tramping overhead to discover the footsteps were actually the thumpings of his own heart caused by indigestion!

The Greek philosophers sought for a rational explanation of dreaming. Aristotle could not accept that the gods contacted men in dreams or that the soul wandered independently during sleep, but allowed that symptoms of some future illness might be seen in a dream. He also believed that dreams might be caused by some mood or activity belonging to waking life, and which the mind still dwelt upon while the body slept. As for divining the future, Aristotle gave a sensible if rather unexciting explanation: that there are so many different kinds of dreams some of them are bound to coincide with actual future events. Plato foreshadowed certain modern theories when he wrote that during sleep those actions normally repressed in thought and deed break through to produce violent and lustful dreams of murder, unlawful sexual activity, or sacrilege.

The Roman world held all forms of divination in great esteem. There are plenty of accounts of dreams relating to the deaths of emperors. Julius Caesar's wife, Calpurnia, is said to have dreamed of his assassination the night prior to his murder. Nero seems to have been afflicted with unpleasant dreams suggesting that the imperial mind feared its body might come to a nasty end!

The Roman republican philosopher, Cicero, wrote a book called *On Divination* in which he demonstrated a sceptical and sophisticated attitude to all divine dreams. Unlike other Romans he wondered why the gods should choose to warn men in such an unreliable way, and how anyone could ever really tell which were the 'true' or 'false' dreams.

It is ironic that this Roman who doubted the accepted dream code owed his own destruction in part to having taken one dream very seriously. It depicted Octavius gaining control of Rome. Cicero allied himself to this cause, and when it proved successful he naturally hoped for some reward. The dream, however, had not shown the eventual 'pay-off': that Mark Anthony would succeed with his plea that Cicero and his brother should die.

'...Dreams and visions are infused into men for their advantage and instruction ...' So wrote Artemidorus of Ephesus in the 2nd century AD. This renowned authority on dream interpretation influenced all subsequent centuries of European dream books linking them through his studies to Assyrian, Babylonian, and Egyptian beliefs.

His definitive work *Oneirocritica* was translated into many European languages, and by the mid-18th century had appeared in its twenty-fourth English edition. In it Artemidorus made the first real attempt to bring reason and evidence to oneirology instead of relying upon a mass of unexamined quasi-religious beliefs or philosophical arguments. He saw that it was utterly ridiculous to apply arbitrary interpretation to such an individual process as dreaming, and warned all interpreters against being too facile and logical in explaining a dream.

Both Freud and Jung paid tribute to the painstaking researches made by this Roman savant who covered every aspect of dreaming. But, according to Artemidorus, interpretation depended upon the effect dream images produced in the conscious mind of the *inter-*

preter, who played the major role in oneirology. However, modern psychoanalysis depends on the associations aroused in the mind of the *dreamer*. It is curious to note here that ancient Indian and Chinese theories of interpretation, unlike contemporary near-Eastern and European counter-parts, shared this modern attitude.

Though Artemidorus's writing might sound naïve or limited by today's thinking, which naturally cannot escape its conditioning from everyday scientific knowledge, certain of his interpretations of the major dream symbols closely resemble those found in psychoanalysis.

A mouth represents a house, and the teeth were its inhabitants, so that dreams of losing teeth express a fear of, or wish for, the removal of someone close to the dreamer. Dreams of sowing and tilling the soil still refer to the desire for marriage and children; for a field represents a woman and seeds are offspring. Artemidorus preceded Freudian thought by nearly two thousand years when he wrote that dreams of excrement and mud signify wealth and treasure, an interpretation also to be found in the Assyrian Book of Dreams.

In assessing dreams, Artemidorus divided them into two categories. The first was fairly simple, and related to those which were the fruits of conditions present in the dreamer's body and mind. So a thirsty man would dream of drink, and someone in love of the beloved person.

The second type was far more complex, and obvi-

ously its interpretation depended upon the oneiro‑
critic's skill. These were dreams referring to the future.
They were often beyond the dreamer's understanding,
and contained symbols which might yield verbal or
visual puns to complicate their meaning even further.
Anyone accustomed to wrestling with cryptic cross-
word clues will have some idea of the difficulties involved.

To dream of having a barber cut your hair was considered a good omen for, as Artemidorus explained,
the Greek word for being barbered was very similar
to the word for joy. He also quoted Aristander on a
dream of Alexander the Great, who was besieging
Tyre. The king dreamed of a satyr dancing on his
shield, and Aristander encouraged him to take the city
by explaining that the dream meant 'sa Tyros' – 'Tyre
is thine'!

This concept of word play has not been discarded
with time. Analysts see it as one method by which the
unconscious cloaks its secrets. These puns often lose
their meaning in another language, as you will know
if you've ever tried to tell a typical English joke in
German or French. This may explain why some of the
glib meanings in modern dream books appear to make
no sense whatever . . . especially if they're updated
versions of far earlier manuals, which in turn had
garnered their interpretations from poor and mangled
translations of Greek and Latin.

In interpreting this second type of dream, Artemidorus advised the oneirocritic to consider all factors

known about the dreamer: his name, nature, occupation, character, and if any particular dream occurred regularly. Unfortunately, his interpretations are too numerous to be fully listed here, but these are some which can be compared with dreams mentioned elsewhere in the book.

To dream of snakes signified illness. This is quite logical when we remember that the serpent was the badge of Aesculapius. Rather reasonably, earthquakes foretold a change of situation! Ladders symbolised an elevated position. A married man who dreamed of his own death would be divorced, or separated from his friends, since the dead need neither wife nor friends. But an invalid who dreamed of being dead would recover because the dead are no longer sick.

To dream of big, beautiful birds was a good omen for important men, and small birds predicted good for the lowly. Flying dreams gave a promise of happiness, wealth, and fame, just so long as the dreamer landed easily and woke immediately, but it was unfavourable to dream of flying head downwards. A mirror signified the opposite sex to the dreamer, but any reflection seen on water foretold the death of the dreamer or one of his family – there's more than a hint of the legend of Narcissus in this interpretation.

We can see why Artemidorus considered it so important to take into consideration details of the dreamer's actual life:

To see oneself crucified is a good portent for those who navigate and for men short of money; those, on the other hand, who have plenty of money will have afflictions and disappointments from this dream; bachelors will see in it a promise of marriage, serfs a promise of liberty. To see oneself crucified in a public establishment or monument is a sign that one will be in charge of, or hold the office inherent in this establishment or monument . . . for example, the dreamer crucified in a school will become a teacher, and he who sees himself crucified in a church will take holy orders . . .

Some of his meanings have much in common with ones described by modern anthropologists working among African tribes as yet unmarked by scientific thought. This presents an interesting example of how not only dreams, but also their interpretations, can link people of totally different centuries, continents, and religious teachings. We know what Artemidorus said about losing a tooth. In Africa a similar dream means the loss of a wife or child. For both Artemidorus and the tribesman floods predict misfortunes in legal matters, and bad-tempered employers. For the Roman, a fire in the sky foretold war; for the African, a bush fire signifies the same thing . . .

Indian and Chinese cultures explained not only dreams, but trances, visions, and hallucinations as the result of the soul leaving the body to explore domains barred to it during waking hours. The Hindu Atharva Veda listed dreams as 'good' or 'bad'. Aggressive symbols and blood were 'good', even if the dream portrayed the dreamer's blood being shed by a sword while he was fighting. However, it was a 'bad' dream if his image accepted death without any struggle. Once again, contrary interpretations appear: sorrow predicted happiness, death predicted long life.

An intriguing feature of Hindu oneirology was the use of dreams to recognise temperaments and physical types, of which they only allowed for three. The bilious man dreamed of golden landscapes, yellow temples, red flowers, forest fires, and suffering from heat; he was always seeking cool places to bathe and drink. A phlegmatic type dreamed of rivers, snow, mist, moonlight, yellow and white plants, and swans. The sanguine person had dreams of racing clouds, hurricanes, restless herdsmen and flocks of migratory birds.

Ancient China was extremely interested in dreaming and oneirology. To interpret successfully it was believed that time, season, the position of the sun, earth, moon, and stars had all to be taken into consideration. The Chinese held that to know the cause of bad dreams expelled fear and worry. Physical factors often played a large part in explaining a dream: so if you fell asleep on a belt you might very well dream of a snake.... If you were hungry you'd dream of taking, but if sated, of giving. Once again, opposites appear in interpretation: dreams of singing and dancing foretold grief. Taoist philosophers were concerned about the nature of reality: could the life led in dreams be real, and what we take for living, in fact, only be the dream?

Chuang-tzu, writing in the 3rd century BC, gives a charming example of such a question about dreams.

'One night I dreamed I was a butterfly, fluttering hither and thither, content with my lot. Suddenly I awoke and I was Chuang-tzu again. Who am I in reality? A butterfly dreaming that I am Chuang-tzu or Chuang-tzu imagining he was a butterfly?'

When Christianity engulfed Europe it absorbed many of the existing pagan customs, giving them a Christian veneer. Sacred places dedicated to the old gods became saintly shrines. At first, special churches were given over to incubation, and saints instead of pagan deities appeared to help the afflicted in their dreams as the result of previous prayers. Because of biblical authority the Church was forced to accept that some dreams were divinely inspired, and even St Thomas Aquinas concluded that divination through dreams could not be contrary to theology.

Gradually, owing to their divinatory nature, dreams became associated with sorcery, witchcraft, and occultism, and the Church claimed that most of these nocturnal visions were sent by the arch-enemy Satan, whose legion of worshippers had to be eradicated.

The appalling witch-hunting mania that flared up in the 15th century was, not surprisingly, accompanied by a violently repressive attitude towards sex – another of the Devil's snares. It's no news to anyone living at this end of the 20th century that if a natural impulse is totally restricted it must find some way to escape. There were countless reports of the lascivious – and unwelcome – visits paid by male and female demons to defenceless sleepers . . . which was how the people of that unenlightened and unhappy age explained their sexual dreams.

In the horrific witchcraft trials of that era delusion was synonymous with actuality. If a witch claimed she had anointed herself with flying ointment, and then flown on a broomstick to revel at an unholy sabbat presided over by the devil, she was considered guilty ... even though evidence from witnesses proved that the deluded creature had really fallen into a deep, troubled sleep after smearing on the salve. Thus a mere dream could result in torture and execution.

These flying ointments – devoid of their 'eye of newt and toe of frog' ingredients – contained what we now term hallucinogenic substances – such as henbane, belladonna, morning glory seeds, and poppy heads – and were probably similar to the potions administered for incubation in the pre-Christian world. This hints that the individual unconscious seeks out the dreams it most requires to satisfy its deepest yearnings.

Modern theories suggest that often in dreams the mind compensates for something lacking in real life. No doubt the stifled and ignorant peasants of the witchcraft centuries achieved some brief thrill out of dreams which attested they possessed a power to be feared, and could produce such momentous reactions in a court of apparently learned men – even though these revelations entailed the dreamer's own destruction. The hysterical, rumour-laced atmosphere donated enough material for the mind to develop during sleep.

People visited the medieval, so-called sorcerer to obtain salves to apply to their eyelids to induce diabolical dreams . . . or sweet scents with which to anoint their pillows to encourage dreams of love. If verbena and bay leaves do promote dreams as pleasant as their aromas, then I'd rather not experience whatever 'cat's brain and bat's blood enclosed in copper' invokes.

As the centuries passed, magic and its allied interests were superseded by more reasoned attempts at science and medicine. Dreams and their interpretations were no longer of particular interest to the educated minds. Belief in their portents was considered as only suitable for the superstitious who, to judge by the popularity of dream manuals based on the works of Artemidorus, formed a large part of the population. Among simple country folk predictive dreams were especially significant on certain dates like Hallow'een, Midsummer's Eve, and St Agnes Eve. On such nights maidens believed they would be granted a vision of their future husbands in a dream if they followed age-old rituals, which varied with countries. Sleeping with a piece of wedding cake beneath your pillow is a remnant of such romantic superstitions.

We are given a beautiful and poetic image of how girls once prepared for these predictive dreams in Keats' *The Eve of Saint Agnes*.

They told her how, upon St Agnes Eve,
Young virgins might have visions of delight,
And soft adorings from their loves receive
Upon the honeyed middle of the night,

If ceremonies due they did aright;
As supperless to bed they must retire.
And couch supine, their beauties, lily white;
Nor look behind, nor sideways, but require
Of Heaven with upward eyes for all that they desire.

Naturally, the stuff of dreams was minutely explored by artists following a tradition set by antiquity, but this only helped denigrate the subject further in minds seeking rational explanations to all known phenomena. Dreaming was irrational and nebulous, and therefore could not readily lend itself to the 19th century's general craze for scientific research. Informed minds assumed its origins to be physiological: heat, cold, external noises, indigestion were the progenitors of dreams rather than gods or demons. For many years the experiments carried out by the Frenchman, Alfred Maury, were widely cited to uphold this theory.

In his book *Le sommeil et les rêves*, published in 1861, Maury described some fascinating tests he'd carried out to prove that external stimuli unlocked forgotten memories which gave the foundations to dreams.

A feather tickling his face provoked dreams of ghastly facial torture; the aroma of eau de cologne induced a dream of a perfume shop in Cairo. The faint ringing sound made by striking tweezers held close to his ears gave Maury a dream of bells sounding the alarm during the Paris Revolution of 1848.

Maury dreamed of the French Revolution, being tried and condemned to death . . . he felt the guillotine descend ... and awoke to discover the bed rail had fallen across his neck. This seemed to demonstrate just how swiftly touch could be transformed into a dream fantasy.

Maury echoed Plato in his belief that dreams took man back to his natural state, divesting him of those civilised conditionings like honour and conscience, where he could surrender to all his basest desires, untrammelled by fear or sorrow.

Havelock Ellis perceived that emotions were somehow intensely magnified by dreams and required heightened drama to express them. Thus a sleeping man, sweating freely, dreamed of being tortured by savages in response to the faint tickling sensations produced by his own trickles of sweat.

Ellis offered a selection of both physical and mental causes for those flying dreams: the internal respiratory movements, or pumping heart muscles in conjunction with the normal supine sleeping position; or, a memory of a childhood wish; or, the pre-birth floating sensation; or, even some dim recollection of man's primordial fishlike ancestry.

The same year as Maury's book appeared a German, Karl Scherner, published *The Life of Dreams* which was much admired by Freud who later developed some of his ideas. In general, Scherner accepted the physiological explanation, and thought that analysis of the fantasies would reveal their origin.

He saw that dreams allowed completely unrestricted activity for the imagination, and in order to describe the images pictorially it employed a symbolic language. A headache might produce a dream about a ceiling covered with gruesome spiders. The dream language might represent a penis by a pipe, or a clarinet, and a narrow courtyard surrounded by houses could symbolise the space between female thighs...

Around this time too, psychiatric research had shown that sometimes dreams and psychoses had, as Freud wrote, 'the characteristics of being fulfilments of wishes'.

The stage is now set for the entrance of the man who believed that dreams were 'the royal road to the unconscious...'

2

'*The Guardians of Sleep*'

So far our search to understand the meaning and causes of dreams has lead us along the diverse paths of religion, magic, medicine, and superstition. It is time to enter the complex world of psychoanalysis that dawned with the beginning of the 20th century.

Sigmund Freud's *The Interpretation of Dreams* is now regarded as his greatest book, as well as being a classic work of human thought. So it seems incredible that after the book's initial publication in 1900 only six hundred copies were sold in eight years. Subsequently many of his theories formed the foundation for others, or were modified . . . or flatly rejected in favour of later ideas. But the influence of the father of psychoanalysis on the entire subject of dreaming can never be underestimated.

The enormous book makes fascinating reading, even when its critics point out paradoxes, discrepancies, and inconclusive areas . . . or that Freud only chose to answer the questions he was prepared to ask, and skated over certain factors for personal reasons. We are still bound to admire the author's humanity, humour, and sincere enthusiasm as well as his reasoned arguments. Freud presents people as being ultra-human, and includes himself in that description by making use of revealing admissions about his own dreams and memories.

While compiling his patients' dreams Freud was undergoing a period of extreme anxiety. At a vital juncture in his career he had chosen to pioneer a set of revolutionary concepts about dreaming which went right against establishment thinking. He was brave enough to test his own theories to discover the root of his personal neurosis – a painful business for any really aware person to attempt. In studying his dreams, Freud re-discovered hidden childhood memories, which provoked thoughts and feelings he had not been aware existed in himself, including an ambivalent attitude to his father.

He went as far as using one of his own dreams as a specimen to demonstrate his theory of interpretation. The famous dream can be found in very complex detail in *The Interpretation of Dreams* and is known as 'Irma's Injection'. It was partly provoked by the visit of a colleague, Otto, who told Freud that a lady patient Freud had been treating was not yet completely better. This dream was about the patient, Irma, whom Freud had been having difficulty in treating, his own anxieties, his attitude towards Otto and other colleagues; and according to him showed that Otto, not he, was responsible for Irma's poor condition. A highly intricate chain of thought and memory resulted from his interpretation of each part of the dream – some of which Freud refused to pursue because he considered it too indelicate. But he was convinced that the principle behind the dream's content was the fulfilment of a wish, and its motive was that wish, i.e. that it wasn't his fault Irma's condition had remained unsatisfactory.

At a time when the serious-minded were claiming that dreams were mere 'froth', or only induced by external stimuli, Freud chose to risk his professional reputation – made further precarious because he was Jewish and therefore rather an outsider – by expounding a theory which corresponded with the popular belief of his own and all other ages: that the dream *does* contain a meaning. Others may have anticipated some of Freud's beliefs, and provided the basis for certain ideas, but he was the first to attempt to give a complete reason for the dream, its process, use, and how it could be understood.

Opponents insisted that Freud's ideas were unscientific, only applicable to patients suffering from neuroses, and even downright disgusting. The very opposition that Freud and his followers encountered suggested in fact that he was on the right track. For he was saying that everybody possessed a mind with a conscious, a pre-conscious, and an unconscious, and that the last two areas repressed painful memories and feelings. In attempting to reject these new ideas, the psychologists and doctors exemplified the fact that nobody wants to have their hidden longings made known, or even admit to having any . . . or learn that beneath their controlled adult life lurks unanswered desires and childhood frustrations.

The greater the opposition the more dogmatically Freud defended his ideas . . . ideas which poured light on to a lot of dark, distressing areas of thought, and tore down the cobwebs of hypocrisy which were snarling up contemporary middle-class minds. With the prevailing, free-speaking climate fostered by mass-media, it is becoming increasingly difficult for most of us to imagine anyone being hostile towards theories because they contained serious references to universal sexual desires and problems.

Now, of course, it has become almost an old joke to say something is full of tremendous Freudian implication if we can discover the slightest sexual innuendo in an object, word, or action. Thus one of Freud's most important concepts has been adopted, familiarised, and lost much of its significance and impact, which may mean it has served its original purpose by making us aware that in the mind anything can be other than it seems by conscious or unconscious association. Obviously we find it odd that people could have been shocked when Freud suggested that sharp, pointed, apparently sexless objects seen in dreams symbolised the penis, while everyday containers and buildings were really female genitals.

We should remember that Freud never claimed that all dreams have a sexual meaning, but he did write:

'The more one is concerned with the solution of dreams the more one is driven to recognise that the majority of the dreams of adults deal with sexual material and give expression to erotic wishes.'

It is worthwhile to bear in mind that Freud was dealing with patients who had been strictly conditioned about their bodies and emotions. Sex was not a topic for discussion, or thought. Freud's own theories about sexuality horrified his critics, for he believed that babies and little children, instead of being doll-like creatures without the so-called baser instincts, were human beings, and therefore capable of loves, hatreds, frustrations, feelings of being rejected, and sexual sensations . . .

In dealing with his patients' neuroses – anxiety, phobias, obsessions – and hysterical symptoms – dizziness, paralysis, and heart spasms – for which there was no physical cause whatsoever, Freud had discovered that these were actually physical and mental expressions of some deeply-hidden, unbearable memory.

Just so long as the patient was plagued by the neurosis he would not recall the real anguish, which Freud believed had its source in some childhood experience, and generally involved something sexual. Since we know how the Victorians felt about that subject we can't be too astonished to learn that a mind so rigorously conditioned must do anything to prevent the memory from manifesting, and employs a personal censor – the pre-conscious – to prevent this irregular material from making itself known to the conscious.

Freud's concept of the unconscious mind was not
new. However, unlike his predecessors, he believed
that the conscious was the very tip of a huge iceberg
concealed by deep, dark waters. The large hidden
area was the unconscious, which really controls our
thoughts and actions, without the knowledge of the
conscious mind.

In this unconscious, thought is divested of all its
civilised training, and is ruled by instinctive and
sexual forces. This means that the unconscious reverts
to the uncontrolled childhood state ... rather like the
time before we'd been taught not to kick, bite, scream,
or perform our natural functions whenever we chose.
Freud argued that the unfinished problems and unsatisfied desires of early childhood continually patrol
the unconscious, forever seeking instances in everyday
life when they can reappear to seek out again the un-
attained gratification. Between conscious and unconscious is the pre-conscious, which tries to prevent or
distort material escaping from the unconscious mind.

During what he termed periods of 'free-association'
Freud encouraged his patients to talk freely, which
meant allowing the mind to wander as it chose, so that
the subject could relate whatever suggested itself.
Often this treatment led people back to their memories
to trace the original source of problems. During this
'free-association' patients recalled their dreams ...
and these touched off further avenues of recollections
for exploration.

Freud's theory about dreaming was not an offshoot

of his studies of psychoanalysis, but the all-important kernel. Rather like the oneirocritics of old, he believed that the fact of a dreamer discovering the original cause of his dream would help dispel the basic problems. Freud thought it was rare that any single dream could point the way, nor should dreams be interpreted without a knowledge of the dreamer's background, character, and overt troubles.

From his observations Freud was unable to accept that a dream has an entirely physiological source. He held that those basic desires dwelling in the unconscious tried to attain consciousness during sleep. In order to prevent them disturbing the sleeper physically and psychologically, the dream is the process of 'venting' instinctive impulses. These are further masked with symbols, and also through the censorship device of the pre-conscious.

For Freud dreams were the 'guardians of sleep'. If some external stimulus affected the dreamer it was woven into the dream to prevent awakening, and prolong sleep, even if only for a moment.

A man disturbed by the sound of a carpet being beaten immediately dreamed that he had written a play with a certain plot, that it was put on at a theatre, and the first act was greeted with tumultuous applause. How many of us have overslept, simply because our dreams have borrowed the insistent ringing of the alarm clock, so that some part of the mind can think: 'Oh well, it's only a dream. I don't have to get up yet . . .'

Sometimes, if we are hungry, or thirsty, or deprived of tobacco, or want to perform a natural function, we dream of favourite meals, long cool drinks, stacks of cigarettes, or that the visit to the lavatory has been made.

In anxiety dreams, Freud pointed out that if the censorship mechanism couldn't cope with the memories evading it, the dream comes to an end by waking up the person. But, generally, it is the censor that allows us to go on sleeping by disguising the repressed memories.

Freud cites an amusing example of the dream trying to prolong sleep, and the external stimulus becoming so intense that the dream images finally forced the sleeper to waken.

A French nursemaid's sleep was disturbed by her small charge calling out that he wanted to go to the lavatory...

In her dream she is taking the little boy for a walk, and can fulfil his demand by leading him to a wall where he can urinate...

Gradually, the pool of urine grows and grows. It floods the town. It becomes a river with boats, and then a sea with ships sailing on it. The enormity of this flood in the dream eventually woke her up to deal with the crying child.

According to Freud all dreams do in some way fulfil a wish. The easiest examples to demonstrate this theory are by children's dreams. Here, Freud explained that fulfilled wishes are generally connected with some event, surrounded by intense emotion for the child, which took place on the day before the dream.

The day before this dream, Hermann, a little boy of twenty-two months, had been made to give his uncle a present of a basket of fresh cherries, but he'd only been allowed to taste one sample. However, in his dream Hermann ate *all* the cherries.

A little girl went for a walk with her father. As it was getting late they had to turn back before their intended destination. On the way back the child saw a signpost pointing to a place her father had also promised to take her to some other time. That night she dreamed she had in fact visited *both* so-far-un-reached places.

Another little girl, visiting a relative, was put to sleep in an unusually large bed. That night she dreamed the bed was actually far too small for her. Freud pointed out that children often yearn to be big, and since the size of the real bed was a reminder of her littleness she corrected this matter in her dream.

All very simple with children, we might say, but Freud insisted that adult dreams are also about wish-fulfilment. On the whole, though, they are far more complex than the unambiguous dreams of childhood, even if they do contain very brief, easily understood patches.

One of Freud's patients dreamed:

I wanted to give a supper party, but I had nothing in the house but a little smoked salmon. I thought I would go out and buy something, but remembered then that it was Sunday afternoon and all the shops would be shut. Next I tried to ring up some caterers, but the telephone was out of order. So I had to abandon my wish to give a supper party ...

On quick examination, this would suggest that the dream couldn't be the fulfilment of the woman's wish, since it had done precisely the opposite.

However, Freud's analysis showed otherwise. The day before the dream his patient had visited a girl friend, of whom she was jealous, because she felt her husband admired her. This friend was thin, and her husband preferred women with well-rounded figures. The friend had mentioned her desire to put on weight, and during their conversation had said 'When will you invite us over? You always give such lovely food. . . .' The meaning of the dream began to clarify immediately the patient recalled all this. It was as if her dream had retorted: 'I'd rather not have any more dinner parties than invite you over so you can eat, get plump, and attract my husband!'

Freud divided dreams into three categories. The ones in the first category are the simplest, for they make sense and we can understand the motives behind them. The night before a holiday, or some eagerly anticipated occasion, people frequently dream that they've already arrived at their destination, or are attending the longed-for party or theatre ...

The second type of dream has a comprehensible content, but puzzles us because we can't see how it fits in with our thoughts. For instance, you might dream of some well-liked relative dying, when there is no reason to expect, fear, or assume such an event.

The third kind of dream is the really baffling one, in which the events are disconnected and apparently meaningless. Freud considered that the majority of dreams belong in this category.

Now let us look at how Freud believed a dream worked by examining the processes through which he arrived at his interpretations. He held that the dream contains two distinct areas: the manifest and the latent. The manifest is what we recall of our dreams. The latent is the repressed or unconscious wish which produces the manifest – it is the dream thought.

This is clearly demonstrated with those simple first category dreams. The manifest content is that we have arrived at our holiday destination, or theatre or party. The latent is our longing for the arrival, or special date. In overtly sexual dreams, we are often surprised by the manifest which shows us indulging in activities involving other people we couldn't normally accept during waking life. The dream is then a fulfilment of a desire we wouldn't consciously admit to having.

Freud considered that some part of the manifest dream was always related to an event in the near past, usually on the previous day. If it seemed very trivial, then free-association would reveal its nature. Further, deeper association would gradually uncover its links with a more deeply repressed experience belonging to the distant past. This was why he encouraged dreamers to report any detail or memory no matter how unimportant it might seem.

To interpret the manifest Freud studied how the dream worked particularly in relation to categories two and three. When a dream doesn't seem to make much sense, the images should be read, not just as they appear, but as if they were parts of a charade made up of pictures.

Two images that seem to have no relation to each other may be pictorial syllables forming the name of a place, person, or even some book or film, which has a significant bearing on repressed memories.

Here is a very simple example. Perhaps you recall two snatches of a dream. The first is reminiscent of the movie *Camelot* . . . men in shining armour riding chargers in a medieval tournament. The second scene is quite different and mundane . . . it is rush-hour, and you're driving across Waterloo Bridge. Together the two pictures make no sense. They seem to suggest that either a vital part has been forgotten, or that this particular dream just doesn't mean anything. However, a closer examination of your memories might reveal that once you knew someone important in your life who you used to meet outside *Knightsbridge* underground . . .

Since dreams are pictorial, they have to represent abstract concepts visually, which is another reason why the manifest contents may seem bizarre. Perhaps you know someone you like a lot, but who doesn't seem to return your friendship, and acts *coldly* towards you. In your dream the abstract characteristic you attribute to this person becomes a reality, and you see an image of that person standing in the snow.

For Freud our incoherent dreams were the result of five special mechanisms: condensation; displacement; representation; symbolisation; secondary elaboration.

Condensation. In general, it takes little more than half a page to describe the manifest contents of quite a complicated dream. However, once interpretation begins, the dream content expands as the latent factors are revealed. Meanings appear behind meanings until what had first seemed like unmatching pieces in a jigsaw becomes an epic film, which might start with your own birth and range over countless experiences you weren't consciously aware of having . . .

Displacement. In order that the repressed memory can get past the mind's censorship, it adopts an unrecognisable form. Unpleasant or hurtful feelings were attached to a substitute object instead of the original real one. There can't be many people who went through childhood without sometimes feeling totally thwarted by the omnipotent, authoritarian world of parents. Perhaps a mother prevented her child from doing something that seemed vitally important at the time to the child. The infant might have felt a violent desire to kill its mother and thus remove the obstacle to its wishes.

It sounds a horrific idea, but after all little children do frequently yell during some tantrum 'I'm going to kill you . . .', and most of us must have said or felt at some time in adulthood: 'I could cheerfully have murdered so-and-so . . .' when someone has ruined our cherished plans.

The unconscious presents this childish violent wish in disguised terms, and the adult might have an apparently meaningless dream in which he is breaking a doll.

Freud quoted the following dream to demonstrate how displacement can be adapted for disguising repressed wishes. A girl dreamed of seeing her sister's only surviving child dead in the same surroundings as some years previously she had seen the dead body of her sister's first child. She felt no pain about this scene, but totally rejected the idea that the dream represented any wish of hers.

Gradually, interpretation showed that it was beside the other child's coffin she had encountered the man she loved. If the second child died she would probably have a chance of seeing the man again. She longed for the meeting, but resisted this feeling.

The dream had been provoked because the day before she had bought a ticket for a lecture given by the man she still loved. In order to disguise this longing from her the situation was displaced on to an event which was obviously unsuitable for producing happiness.

Anxiety in dreams is often aroused even by the

disguised fulfilment of a repressed wish, especially if the original repression was necessary to spare the person's guilt, fear, or pain. So that to dream of smashing a doll might make the dreamer feel unaccountably unhappy or worried, although on waking the incident would seem too trivial to worry about.

Representation. Dream images represent specific ideas rather than abstractions. Concepts like 'either or' cannot be expressed. In a dream the alternatives must appear as of equal importance. The contents can depict two instances, but cannot supply the conjunction.

Visual images are unable to express the ideas conveyed in words like 'as if', 'because', 'although'. Cause and effect may appear as one scene following on another. The dream cannot explain that the second happened because of the first. Only interpretation can reveal just what the unconscious is trying to say in these instances.

All kinds of essential expressions and feelings cannot be presented pictorially. 'You make me sick' would have to be shown quite literally as the dreamer suffering a bilious attack. 'I feel trapped' might be conveyed by depicting the dreamer within some imprisoning situation ... perhaps lost in the maze at Hampton Court, or behind prison bars, or in manacles chained to a wall. The idea of a situation out of control might appear in a dream as driving a car along a winding road with a deep ravine on one side and a high cliff on the other. As you drive you find that neither steering nor brakes respond, and you're trapped in a crazily jolting vehicle which must hurtle you towards destruction . . .

Symbolisation. In order that a dream which expresses some erotic desire can get past the censor the images must be replaced by apparently non-sexual symbols. Freud warned that the interpretation of these symbols required great caution, and the list he gives in *The Interpretation of Dreams* is extensive.

Freud held that these symbols frequently contained more than one meaning, which made their translation a very tricky ambiguous business. He was anxious that the interpreter should not abandon the use of the dreamer's own free-association in favour of an arbitrary application of reading the symbols. The two methods were meant to be complementary to each other.

'. . . The Emperor and Empress (or the King and Queen) as a rule represent the dreamer's parents; and a Prince or Princess represents the dreamer himself or herself . . .' Really great men can also play the role of father figure in dreams.

. . . All elongated objects, such as sticks, tree trunks and umbrellas (the opening of these last being comparable to an erection), may stand for the male organ – as well as all long, sharp weapons, such as knives, daggers, and pikes . . .

. . . Boxes, cases, chests, cupboards and ovens represent the uterus, and also hollow objects, ships and vessels of all kinds. Rooms in dreams are usually women; if the various ways in and out of them are represented, this interpretation is scarcely open to doubt. . . . A dream of going through a suite of rooms is a brothel or a harem dream . . .

Conversely, Freud pointed out that the same dream can represent marriage.

. . . Steps, ladders or staircases, or, as the case may be, walking up and down them, are representations of the sexual act . . .

Smooth walls over which the dreamer climbs, the facades of houses, down which he lowers himself – often in great anxiety – correspond to erect human bodies, and are probably repeating in the dream recollections of a baby's climbing up his parents or nurse . . .

. . . Since bed and board constitute marriage, the latter often takes the place of the former in dreams and the sexual complex of ideas is, so far as may be, transposed on to the eating complex. As regards articles of clothing, a woman's hat can very often be interpreted with certainty as a *man's* genital organ . . .

. . . In men's dreams a neck-tie often appears as a symbol for the penis. No doubt this is not only because neck-ties are long, dependent objects and peculiar to men, but also because they can be chosen according to taste – a liberty which, in the case of the object symbolised, is forbidden by Nature. Men who make use of this symbol in dreams are often very extravagant in ties in real life and own whole collections of them . . .

. . . all weapons and tools are used as symbols for the male organ, e.g. ploughs, hammers, rifles, revolvers, daggers . . .

. . . Children in dreams often stand for genitals. . . . Playing with a little child, beating it, etc., often represents

masturbation in dreams. To represent castration symbolic-
ally, the dream-work makes use of baldness, hair-cutting,
falling out of teeth and decapitation. If one of the ordinary symbols for a penis occurs in a dream doubled or multi-
plied, it is to be regarded as a warding off of castration. ...
Many of the beasts which are used as genital symbols in
mythology and folklore play the same part in dreams, i.e.
fishes, snails, cats, mice (on account of the pubic hair), and
above all those most important symbols of the male organs
– snakes. Small animals and vermin represent small children – for instance, undesired brothers and sisters. Being
plagued with vermin is often a sign of pregnancy ...

... The genitals can also be represented in dreams by
other parts of the body: the male organ by a hand or a
foot, and the female genital orifice by the mouth, or an
ear, or even an eye. The secretions of the human body –
mucus, tears, urine, semen, etc. – can replace one another
in dreams ... what in fact happens is that significant
secretions, such as semen, are replaced by indifferent
ones ...

After reading this intriguing list it should be obvious
why Freud recommended caution in the use of
symbols.

Secondary Elaboration. This is the final stage of dream
work. On waking, the mind tries to recall the dream,
and adds or subtracts certain elements. This process
is continued when the patient recounts the dream.
Freud found great significance in any areas where particular details varied with each re-telling of the dream.

This was the part of the dream that analyst and patient should examine carefully,

Now, let us examine what are called 'typical dreams, and see how Freud interpreted them, remembering that he claimed no dream could have a general meaning ... only that the raw material for the sensations contained in it is always derived from the same source.

Dreams of being scantily dressed, or stark naked, and walking down the main street among a crowd of uncaring strangers are typical, so long as they are accompanied by a sense of embarrassment, as well as an inability to correct the situation. Freud interprets such dreams as memories of earliest childhood, when you were displayed, and permitted to run around before everyone in your birthday suit. Then there comes the time when the child is told he or she can't run around like that ... and so has to unlearn a behaviour pattern. The dream is a desire for display, and perhaps that original scolding caused a general self-consciousness and reserve in adulthood. In the dream, the individual can return to the time when he was free to be naked whenever he chose, but the censorship begins to demand that this exhibitionism be stopped, hence the guilt feelings.

Dreams of flying or floating, according to Freud, are derived from memories of childhood play, which involved falling sensations, pleasurable fright and giddiness, associated with swings, roundabouts and see-saws, or jumping down flights of stairs. Psychoanalysis, Freud explained, had discovered that the first sexual feelings frequently have their roots in children's games, romping and wrestling.

Typical death dreams are those involving a beloved relative – parent, brother, sister, or child – and are accompanied by real feelings of grief which may well overflow into tears during sleep.

Such dreams, Freud explains, always spring from the dreamer's desire for the death of that particular relative – *not at the time of dreaming*, but from some memory of the dreamer's childhood. The death wishes of children are not really violent or cruel. By 'dead' they mean 'gone away', because that is mainly what we tell them when we try to explain about death.

We know how an only child resents the sudden appearance of a new brother or sister, who is a rival for their parents' attention and affection. The first child will often suggest that the new baby be sent back or thrown away. No doubt the younger child must often wish that the older, bullying brother or sister was also out of the way . . .

Freud gives a rather charming example of a recurring dream on this subject, which was only slightly affected by the dreamer's censorship. The patient was the youngest girl in a large family, and first had this dream when she was four years old: 'A whole crowd of children – all her brothers, sisters and cousins of both sexes – were romping in a field. Suddenly they all grew wings, flew away and disappeared.'

Freud's explanation of a child's desire for the death of a parent is based on what he describes as the

'Oedipus Complex' – that boys are in love with their mothers, are jealous of their fathers, and wish them out of the way so that they can be head of the house, and possess their mothers – and the 'Electra Complex' – that girls see their mothers as rivals for the love of their fathers and want to usurp the other woman's position. This complex theory of infantile sexuality obviously shocked and astounded many people, but the fact that a little child might sometimes want one of its parents out of the way for its own selfish reasons seems quite logical.

All civilisations teach children to love and respect both their parents, and so a child must always feel guilty and ashamed on the occasions when he, or she, has an outburst of hatred against a particular parent.

For a child the parent of the same sex may very well seem a rival for the other parent's love. All little boys learn their first affection for women from loving their mothers, as little girls' first affection for men begins with their love for their fathers. So long as a child develops successfully these feelings are painlessly transferred outside the family.

A boy naturally resents, and even fears, his father's power over him. While father is around it seems he will never be completely a man, and from this sometimes springs the fear of castration. On the other hand, a girl feels frustrated by the rules imposed by her mother, who seems to be preventing her from growing-up.

If we look at children at play, what do we see? Little

girls playing at being housewives, and mothers, and other adult female roles, while little boys pretend to be big tough men and heroes ...

Perhaps we should also remember that a parent tends to be more critical of the child of the same sex. Fathers badger their sons to act like men, and at the same time limit freedom of action, while they often spoil their little girls ... and mothers frequently treat their daughters strictly in an attempt to train them for womanhood, while indulging their little boys, in much the same way that they suffer the whims of grown men.

For these dreams about the death of a parent to get past the censor, the manifest contents can only appear clothed with deepest grief.

Some more typical dreams are in the last section of this book, explained in terms of Freud's and other people's theories.

Freud uncovered the kingdom of dreams, which had been buried beneath the debris of the past, and encouraged other people to explore the subject. His wish-fulfilment theory would have been more acceptable if he had not adhered so strictly to the idea that dreams are mainly related to sexual desires. He didn't appear to realise that the contents of dreams are not only based upon a wish, but also on the problems created by that wish ... nor did he show that the dream could make a more positive and creative contribution to the dreamer's life.

We must remember that Freud never claimed to understand the whole truth. His tremendous discoveries were not so much an answer as a **beginning** ... rather as you might beam a torch into **some unknown** dark territory, and decide that what you **could see in the** arc of light was all that existed. Undoubtedly, **Freud** suffered personally when the brilliant **brains he respected,** and trusted to uphold and develop **his ideas,** began rejecting them to follow their own lights in the darkness. And so the great dispute led to further thought, research and discovery. Freud had laid the invaluable foundation for a scientific study of dreaming ...

3

The Dream Conflict

BY 1914 doctors and psychologists, outside Freud's own group of founder psychoanalysts, had reluctantly begun to accept his approach to the problems affecting the human mind. It was around this time that the rift occurred between Freud and his closest collaborators, springing from personal and professional differences.

Carl Gustav Jung, Alfred Adler, Otto Rank, and Wilhelm Stekel broke away to found their own schools of therapeutic psychology. Since they differed from Freud on theories of psychoanalysis, it was not unnatural that they came to other conclusions about the reason and importance of dreaming.

None of them disagreed with Freud's basic premise that the dream is a significant psychic happening, but they were unconvinced by the meanings he ascribed to dreams, and his methods of interpretation. The theory of wish-fulfilment, and the emphasis on sexual desires in the unconscious did not satisfy them, nor could they see dreams as purely neurotic symptoms mirroring those early recollections and experiences that a person could not surmount or weave into his adult character.

Mainly this heretical group disagreed with his view that the latent aspect of a dream contained the root of its meaning, and that any attempt to interpret the manifest – as in the tradition of all past oneirocritics – was an error.

They considered that the dream, its symbols and content, plus its relation to the dreamer's problems and personality were of supreme relevance. They also argued that Freud had restored significance to the whole process of dreaming, and then practically dismissed it to study the underlying causes, using the manifest content as the merest clue.

The chief dissenter was Carl Jung, born in 1875, the son of a Swiss Protestant minister, and the founder of what is termed the Zurich School. Ironically enough, Freud had regarded him as the heir-apparent to the kingdom he had discovered.

Jung's collection of writings are full of obscure but fascinating mythological, religious, and anthropological allusions, which are an integral part of his theories. They carry us into a vaster, less rigidly defined realm than the one Freud had presented.

In order to understand something of what Jung thought about dreams we must get some idea of how his concepts differed from Freud's.

Firstly, Jung required that the psychoanalyst must undergo psychoanalysis, something that Freud had never experienced. Only through this could a doctor become aware of the motives and causes behind his own approach to a patient's problems and dreams.

In other words – if an analyst harboured some deeply repressed feelings about, let us say, lemons ... and had not been analysed and made aware of his feelings and reasons for having them, any patient who mentioned a dream of a lemon tree might well trigger off all sorts of interesting conjectures and interpretations on the analyst's part, which would relate to his own unknown problems, but have little or nothing to do with the dreamer's.

Obviously it is a truism to point out that Carl Jung and Sigmund Freud were entirely different individuals, utterly dissimilar in background and religion, even though they were linked through their studies of the mind. Most people cannot see all things the same way, especially those abstract matters which cannot be proved scientifically – and some individuals, for instance those who believe the earth is flat, insist on flying in the face of what one would call irrefutable evidence – and we should bear this fact in mind when we consider the opposing points of view about dreams.

All of us are conditioned by our backgrounds, and therefore do not find the same importance in objects or events. If an orthodox Jew dreams of eating pork, something his religion forbids, or a Moslem dreams of drinking alcohol, which his religion forbids along with eating pork, either of their reactions to such dreams are bound to be very different from someone for whom pork or alcohol has no significance whatsoever.

Naturally, such factors affect analysts and patients alike, since both are human beings, which means the analyst has to try to know all there is to know about himself, as well as his patient.

Let us take another example: if a man dreams about a glass of beer, and says it made him feel anxious, it might sound ridiculously unimportant until we know his father had been a staunch teetotaller, who had always told his son that drink was the work of the devil. For someone else it might evoke happy and sad memories of a day spent in a country pub with a past sweetheart ...

As we have seen, Freud deciphered his patients' dream symbols in sexual terms, because this produced a therapeutic answer to their neuroses as well as *his* own undoubted sexual problems to which he only briefly alluded. Sexual repression was a product of the 19th century, and Freud – a man of his own time – tried to cure its ills, so helping liberate civilisation from many agonising taboos. Jung's theories have a greater affinity to the 20th century. After all he only died in 1961. For in seeking the function rather than the cause of dreams, Jung appeared to be looking for the meaning of existence, which is the great question asked by our age. Thus, if unresolved sexual problems colour Freud's dream theories, then it is unresolved spiritual problems which are in the background of Jungian concepts.

Jung found Freud's methods of interpretation too arbitrary, especially in their reliance on sexual symbols. 'An arbitrary interpretation of dreams,' he wrote, 'is absolutely inadmissible. . . .' Freud was opposed to Jung's interpretative theories because they were based too much on intuitive understanding, whereas he had wanted psychoanalysis to be on a strictly scientific basis.

To emphasise his opposition to the Freudian viewpoint Jung quoted the *Talmud*, 'the dream is its own interpretation'. He refused to believe that the manifest content was a façade which disguised the true meaning, merely because it was very difficult to understand the dream. That would be like saying a page of Chinese writing makes no sense, and is therefore obscuring its meaning. The actuality would be that we don't know how to read Chinese. If we want to understand it, then we'd better start learning the characters.

Jung couldn't see why a dream was supposed to be some cunning device to trick the dreamer out of comprehending what his unconscious was saying, and also if the censorship mechanism was so important, why then could it be circumvented?

Since he considered that dreaming was a vital factor in human existence Jung could not allow that the dream, and its interpretation, was only to be associated with neuroses. He denied the dream was merely the fulfilment of a wish, and pointed out that many people had been spurred on to great ambitions and deeds by their dreams making them dissatisfied with life as it was.

As for the dream being the guardian of sleep, Jung

wondered why, if this was really true, dreams were so often instrumental in waking up sleepers. He did not reject Freud's important discoveries about sexuality, but could not accept that sexual desires were the primary causes of dreams. Sex may be one of the strongest human impulses, but there are others which are just as powerful: ambition, religion, patriotism, maternal love, and even altruism . . .

For Jung, each dream was unique to the individual dreamer, and therefore any mechanical method of interpreting dreams through symbols could hardly reveal a meaning for that individual. This method could only be really viable in the case of some universal symbols, which mean the same thing to all men of all centuries. When it came to that extensive list of Freudian sex symbols, Jung wondered why so many of the objects, each with an utterly different function, could represent the same thing.

He considered it necessary to discover what the objects in a dream meant to the dreamer, whom he encouraged to talk about them. This method is known as 'amplification', and certainly doesn't always reduce a gun, a knife, a cigarette, or a lady's hat, to meaning a penis . . . or a stove, a vase, a box, a ship, to meaning a vagina or a uterus.

Amplification is very different from free-association, because it requires that the subject consciously concentrates on the object in question instead of letting his mind wander almost dreamily. He relates everything he knows about it, or what it reminds him of.

1. Hypnos, god of sleep.

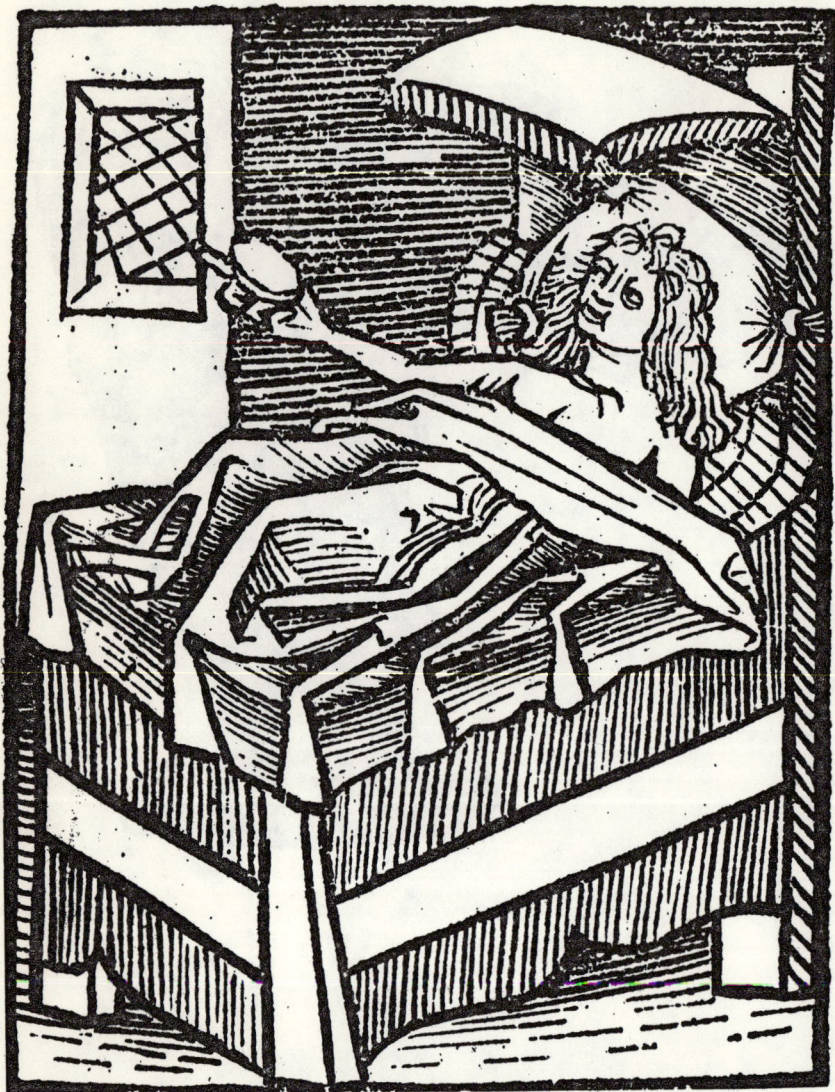

2. A late 15th-century engraving shows a potential dreamer holding a stone, Zizaa, which was said to give marvellous dreams.

3. A 16th-century engraving of a sleepwalker.

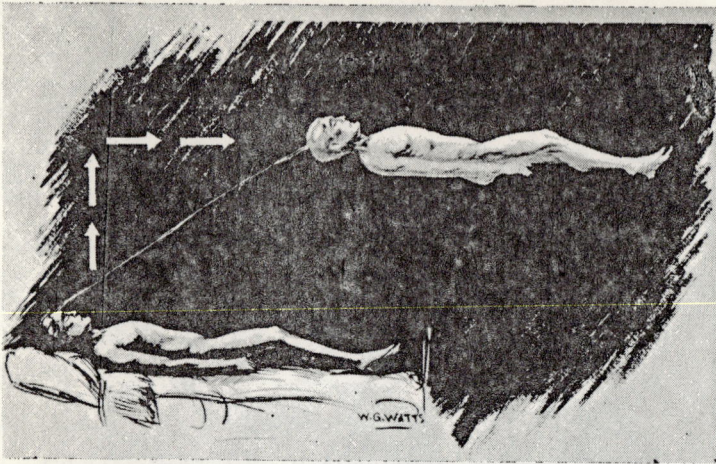

4. *Above*. The astral body lying in the air above the physical body of the dreamer, to which it is connected by an elastic 'cord'. The arrows show the route the astral body takes in projecting. From *The Projection of the Astral Body* by S. Muldoon and H. S. Carrington (Rider, 1929).

5. *Below*. An inscription before the Sphinx at Giza recounts the dream of Thutmose IV.

6. *Above*. Joseph dreaming. A 14th-century Istanbul fresco.
7. *Below*. *Jacob's Dream* by Ribera.

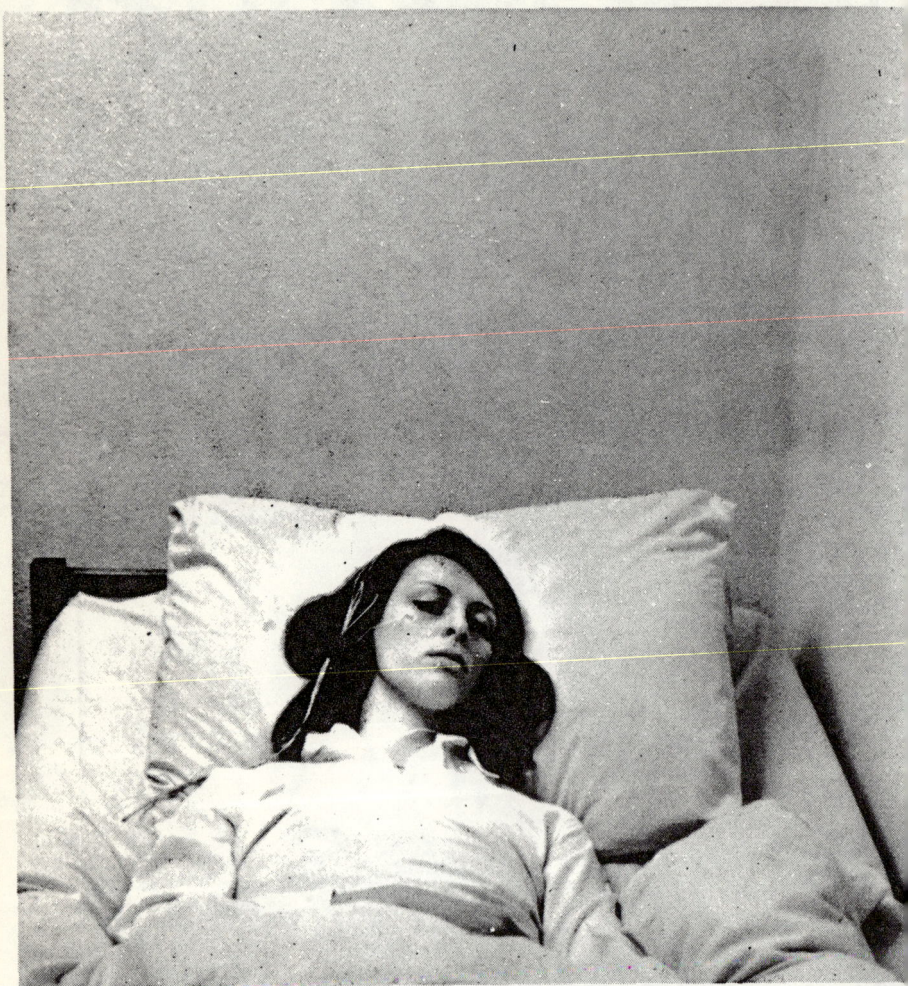

8. A sleeper undergoing an EEG test.

9. This type of photographic montage was popular in the
late 19th century.

10. Back row, left to right, A. A. Brill, E. Jones, S. Ferenczi.
Front row, left to right, S. Freud, S. Hall, C. G. Jung.

Amplification does not intend to lead the dreamer away from the particular object, rather he begins to perceive exactly what it does mean for him.

According to Jung the dream forms a whole, rather like a play in three acts. He was not averse to separating parts of the dream in order to study them more minutely, but he believed that free-association, arising from the fragmentation of a dream, only tended to lead the dreamer further away from his dream.

Free-association to uncover deeply concealed problems didn't need to start from dreams anyhow. Psychoanalysis had devised many other methods, like gazing into a crystal ball and reacting to Rorschach cards, to reveal those characteristics someone might wish to hide. Later, of course, drugs have proved of the greatest value in peeling back layers of the mind in order to bring to light those deeply repressed memories.

Another important Jungian theory was that no one dream could be interpreted by itself. It was necessary to examine a series of dreams, to see if certain features re-occurred, or were always absent. Often, Jung found that one dream seemed to interpret a previous one, just as if the unconscious was trying to find some other terms with which to make itself understood.

Jung believed the unconscious houses a stranger, who speaks to us through our dreams, and tries to tell us how it sees us. Its opinion obviously differs very much from the way we see ourselves, for the stranger practises a kind of internal objectivity, since we have no control over the unconscious. Through this, it can sometimes show that a 'difficult situation' is the result of our own attitudes which require changing. Our problem is to understand the 'stranger's' message, and its link with that 'difficult situation'.

Jung agreed with Freud that the greater part of the self belongs to the realms of the unconscious. However, his own concept of that unconscious area differed from Freud's which was the reason why he viewed dreaming in such a different light.

According to Jung, the unconscious derives its material from universal archaic structures in the brain, and from racial and familial memories. It is like some fantastic kind of computer, able to create infinite permutations, and from this source comes more dream images and thought associations than could ever be created by conscious concentration.

Jung allowed that each individual possesses what he described as a 'personal unconscious', which, as Freud had said, contains material experienced at the conscious level, and then repressed. But for Jung that was not the total of the unconscious. He believed that also within each person there is the 'collective unconscious'.

This contains the universal ancestral experiences, which appear in 'primordial images' Jung explained that through the collective unconscious each human being houses all the truly beautiful and great thoughts, feelings and impulses of humanity, plus every deed of shame and devilry of which man has ever been capable.

Jung claimed that from this source sprang the meaning of man's existence, and those basic preoccupations and experiences which must have always conditioned mankind: birth, life, death, marriage, bravery, evil, murder, hunger, beauty, religion, and the conflicts involved in developing and maturing.

Just as our bodies still carry traces of our ancient aquatic ancestry, so our minds inherit the potentialities of human imagination. Jung called the form in which these 'primordial images' manifest during conscious life 'archetypal images', and their potentialities are 'archetypes' – the patterns of thought found in religions, religious ritual, myths, fairytales, and dreams.

Again and again the similarities emerge, irrespective of time or place, recognisable even though they are conditioned by a variety of languages and customs. We have already noted the likeness between African and ancient Roman dream interpretation.

A hero overcoming some terrible monster represents man's fight against the untamed forces inside himself, and is vividly described in tales like Jack the Giant Killer and St George and the Dragon. A lonely and scorned person is eventually released to be recognised for his or her true worth is a concept found in tales like Cinderella and the Ugly Duckling. Such stories depict universal emotions, problems and longings, and so are naturally repeated all over the world in differing forms.

According to Jung dreams repeat similar ideas, because they are attempting to describe and help make comprehensible our deep and eternal problems. The archetypes expressing these abstract ideas continually appear, and if we could only learn to understand them we should be able to interpret our dreams.

Jung never claimed that these archetypes are inherited, only that the structures which created them are repeated in each individual. The theory must remain hypothetical since we can't yet know what little babies dream about. By the time they can talk, it is impossible to guage whether or not certain dream patterns have been conditioned in them by environment, discipline, and nursery tales.

One of the best known archetypes is the Hero, who can be the Messiah, or the great man of any age, who will save part or all of mankind. Such figures constantly reappear in world religions and political movements to sway millions of human beings for good or ill. Jesus, Mahomet, Lenin, Hitler, and Churchill personify this archetype.

Another well-known archetype is the Great Mother, the perfectly good woman or goddess, who intercedes and saves, as personified by the Virgin Mary and female saints. An opposing archetype is the Terrible Mother, who frequently appears in fairytales and myths. She is the angry goddess, the wicked witch, the nasty step-mother.

Of course children often reflect in their dreams that mother has two aspects: when she is very kind and gentle; and those frightening occasions when, for the child, her anger seems unintelligible and quite dreadful – as if the familiar figure has been transformed into some terrible stranger.

The concept of Sacrifice is also archetypal, and can be found in any century and civilisation . . . that one perfect and good being should be destroyed for the greater good. A comprehensive example of this important archetype appearing in dreams is to be found in John Layard's fascinating study *The Lady of the Hare*. The first part deals with helping a woman to understand her own rich supply of dreams. This in turn directly helped in the development of her backward teenage daughter.

At an important juncture in her own self-understanding and development, the woman dreamed of sacrificing a hare, which showed no resistence to the knife. Mr Layard went on to explain that this hare symbol appeared in many patients' dreams.

The second half of his book describes the mythology of the hare, which appears in different situations in every civilisation, and is a feature of religion and folklore. It was a deity for American Indians, ancient Egyptians, and Anglo Saxons, and a symbol of love and sacrifice, rather like the idea of the Judaic and Christian lamb. Degenerated pockets of this belief can be found in the old English customs of 'killing a hare' on Good Friday, and 'hunting the hare' on Easter Monday. The hare is associated with rebirth, fertility, whiteness, snow, the moon, and is a symbol of intuition. In Europe the folk memory of this creature, like so many ancient religious symbols, became connected with witchcraft. Witches were said to turn themselves into hares, because the animal could move swiftly and therefore seem to disappear ...

We have already seen how the ancient gods of healing were presumed to appear to dreamers in sanctuaries dedicated to healing, and the Healer is another example of the archetype.

For some of his disciples Jung represented the Wise Old Man – the archetypal teacher or spiritual guide, who appears in our dreams as father or prophet – and Jung believed that we must always take the advice given by such a figure, for he symbolises mankind's ancient wisdom and intuition.

According to Jung, the personality contains two archetypes: the 'persona', and the 'shadow'.

The persona is the character or mask we present to the world. It is the kind of person we want people to take us for. To use the expression 'lose face' signifies just what we fear will happen to us in front of others, and that they will glimpse behind our mask.

The shadow is the contrary aspect – our less admirable side, which we hope doesn't show. It appears in dreams as the same sex as the dreamer, and has all the annoying or childish characteristics which we attribute to other folk, but refuse to see in ourselves.

Two other vital archetypes are the 'anima' and 'animus'. The anima appears in a man's dream in female form, and the animus is masculine in a woman's dream. This archetype is related to the vestigial physical characteristics of the opposite sex found in each human being. In order to be whatever our dominant sexual attributes define us as, we repress the counterpart tendencies which then manifest themselves in our dreams.

Yet each person requires their anima or animus to be a completely integrated personality – a whole and balanced person. It is that little bit of leavening in the human bread, and by appearing in our dreams the anima or animus is trying to remind us of this.

Not every female figure in a man's dream is the anima, and the same fact is true of women's dreams, but it is important to remember that the anima and animus can be played by several different characters at one time in a dream.

These natural archetypes were originally represented, according to Jung, by the mythological gods and goddesses. Helen of Troy and Venus personified the concept in the ancient mind, as did the Mother Church and the Virgin Mary for the medieval mind. We could describe the anima as the 'eternal woman', and she can be either a saint or a thorough harlot. A perfect example of the anima used as a literary device is Rider Haggard's *She*.

Men project their anima on to film stars . . . idealised unknown women whom we recognise as having that indefinable 'it' like Garbo, Bardot, or Monroe. Of course, men will also choose a more accessible individual woman, which explains that old idea of 'being attracted by opposites' for, depending on the nature of a man's anima, his 'ideal' woman can be virtuous or promiscuous.

The animus, of course, can be a mixture of hero and rake. We find him in every kind of fiction. He is epitomised by film stars, pop idols, great explorers, strong men, or surgeons.

It is hardly necessary to say that Freud considered that dreams of women by men, or men by women, were an indication of an individual's sexual desires. Jung agreed that this might be true, but it could also be that the unconscious was attempting to guide the individual towards wholeness and fulfilment by making him or her aware of the complementary part of their personality.

Jung believed that the unconscious contains a far greater understanding of the self than is available to the conscious, which can't help being trammelled by those everyday problems. Life requires balance. The ancient Greeks saw long ago that the really great sin was lack of balance, for that is what tips us over into delusion. In order that life follows its proper course it needs equilibrium – love and hate, youth and age, birth and death, joy and sadness. These are not merely opposing concepts. Together they make up a totality. We can't experience one without knowing the others.

Just as the body contains a physical self-regulating system so that we perspire when we are hot, so the unconscious seems to attempt to balance our personality. Jung believed that this means dreams play a compensatory role – something like Freud's theory of wish-fulfilment – but that this compensation process is related to the now rather than those unrealised childhood aspirations.

Jung thought that dreams could help us because they represent what is repressed in the personality, and tell us not just what we *desire*, but what we *need*, to be complete.

This theory that dreams have a compensatory function in some way explains the antique method of interpreting dreams through opposites.

The hard person will dream of being gentle The ultra-tidy will dream of being untidy and messy. The rake will experience guilt. The bully will be a coward. The man who feels inferior and shy might dream of going to Buckingham Palace to meet the Queen; the timid of performing some valorous deed. The plain unnoticed girl might well dream of being a fashion model or a film star. The boy who has difficulty in 'chatting up' the girls may dream he owns a harem. The meek might dominate and be cruel in their dreams . . .

It was Jung who saw that some people were 'introverts' – with tendencies to look inwards and analyse themselves – while others were 'extroverts' – the inveterate party-goers, who seem to feel lacking unless they're part of a crowd. In dreams, however, the extrovert may be deeply introspective, while the introvert may dream of being wildly sociable and gay . . .

So Jung's theory of dream interpretation might reveal not only what the primitive impulses in the collective unconscious are seeking, but also what we need to balance our attitude and personality.

The dream may also reveal what we really feel about a friend or relative. Jung cited an example of a young man, whose sense of inadequacy was the result of a terrifically upright father. In a dream the son saw his father as a drunk. Jung interpreted the dream as meaning that the young man's unconscious was trying to tell him he needn't feel so inferior because his father was less than perfect.

This compensatory process may also allow a dream to indicate factors which had been overlooked in waking life, and so help solve some problem which you may have cudgelled your brain over all the previous day.

Perhaps it is a little unfair to Freud to mention here that a much later authority – Dr J. A. Hadfield, a founder of the Tavistock Clinic in London, and the author of *Dreams and Nightmares* – re-interpreted the dream of 'Irma's Injection' quite differently from its dreamer, with a slant towards Jung's beliefs. He suggested that Freud's interpretation was in fact the fulfilment of a wish, whereas the actual dream stated the problem, and further emphasised Freud's failure to cure Irma by pointing out all sorts of past cases where he'd been unsuccessful. For Hadfield, then, Freud's dream stated the problem, demonstrated its causes, and pointed towards the solution . . .

Jung saw that dreams contained everything that the consciousness rejects, overlooks, and forgets. They were also prospective, and so if their advice could be followed, dreams might, as the ancients believed, be predictive, for they served as signposts towards maturity, revealing a potential which circumstances had probably forced the dreamer to abandon.

Nightmares and bad dreams – that threaten to swamp the sleeper and contain unknown dragons, monsters and vampires, or in which we enter dreadful pitchy caverns, or walk beneath the seas – hark back to primeval times. The images represent the darker emotions: lust and power, guilt, and retribution. They may make us frightened of falling asleep, but Jung considered that such dreams, provided they were correctly interpreted, could be usefully absorbed and integrated into the individual personality.

Since so many of the dream symbols appear in mythology, Jung frequently used myths to help interpret a dream. For instance, the cave appears in many myths, and also in dreams. For Freud it must represent the womb, but Jung saw it as depicting the hidden recess of the unconscious. Often the cave is shown with a snake coming out of it. The Freudian interpretation is quite obvious, but mythology regarded the snake as a symbol of healing or wisdom, and also of re-birth, since a snake sheds its skin. Jung believed that the appearance of a snake in a dream suggests conflict between a conscious attitude and a basic instinct.

For Freud the spider was the symbol of the terrifying mother, who imprisoned her son to prevent him attaining a woman of his own. Observing that the spider is a cold-blooded creature, Jung saw its appearance in dreams as representing the psychic world which is utterly strange to human beings. We know that Freud explained houses as female symbols; for Jung a house in a dream represented the persona covering what takes place within its walls. According to Jung the sea is the symbol of the collective unconscious, since it was from these waters that all mankind originally emerged. For Freud it means the uterine waters and the memory of birth, and perhaps the desire to return to the security of the mother's womb ...

As if in confirmation of Jung's theory of the personal and collective unconscious he discovered that, among certain peoples living in East Africa, whenever a 'big' dream occurred – that is, one which had a general meaning for the other members of the tribe – everyone assembled to hear about it.

Jung felt that those 'meaningful' dreams come from the collective unconscious and are often clothed with beauty and poetic powers. He believed that such dreams mostly occur during significant phases of life, which are accompanied by changes in the psychological condition: early youth, puberty, at the onset of middle age, and within reach of death. He claimed that people approaching death often dream of crossing fords, re-birth, journeys, and moving from place to place.

A simple example of the 'big' dreams is that which appears in many religions, heralding the arrival of a saviour. In the New Testament, Joseph dreamed that an angel appeared, saying:

Joseph, thou son of David, fear not to take unto thee Mary thy wife: for that which is conceived in her is of the Holy Ghost. And she shall bring forth a son, and thou shalt call his name Jesus: for he shall save his people from their sins . . .

Buddha's mother, Maya, dreamed:

White as snow or silver, more brilliant than the moon or the sun, the best of elephants, with fine feet, well-balanced, with strong joints, with six tusks hard as adamant, the magnanimous, the very beautiful has entered my womb. I must understand the meaning of this dream.

The Brahmin soothsayers interpreted her dream as meaning:

. . . A son will be born to Maya; his body will bear the characteristic marks. Issue of a royal line, the magnanimous one will be a universal monarch. He will abandon his capital, the kingdom, all desires of his own home; detached from everything by compassion for the three worlds, he will become a wandering monk. It is he who acts for the good of the three worlds, by the sweetness of his ambrosia, he will be able to satisfy all worlds . . .

In a dream the wife of a great ancient Egyptian magician was told how she could end her barrenness. When she became pregnant her husband had a dream which told him what name to give the child, and that it would be a great magician who would guide and aid his people . . .

Reading Jung, you are struck by the realisation that the interpretation of dreams also requires a balance. Freud's insistence on the original causes being the meaning is compensated by Jung's search for a meaningful end.

He considered that the dream is essentially spiritual, and encompasses all the known and unknown regions of the human psyche. Dreaming is the way by which man tries to find the reason for existence . . . a restatement of all past unresolved problems, and the meeting point between past and future. Jung did not see the archetypes as the remains of an eternal repetition of human experiences. For him, they contained the potential seed of evolution. This would mean that the dream asks something of humanity. The symbols are really the impulses of civilisation, and their images change basic instinct into energy directed towards a better integrated society.

Since the dream is the product of the individual's psyche, Jung held that if we could really comprehend it we should know far more about the whole psychic process. Through that we should become more integrated as individuals, and thus capable of leading a rich and fulfilled life.

In Freud's theories there is a sense of looking back at factors which cannot be altered, and so seem to cripple the future. They might, therefore, quite unintentionally, lead people to despair. With Jung there is the feeling of looking forward ... of learning through our dreams, and mankind's experiences, to be a happier person.

Now let us look at two dreams frequently quoted to demonstrate the differences between the Jungian and Freudian approaches to interpretation. A young man dreamed he was in an unknown garden. He plucked an apple from a tree, and looked around to make sure no one saw him.

The dreamer admitted he had begun an affair with a maidservant, and had a meeting with her the day before the dream. He could see the mythological symbolism associated with the garden and the apple, but the dream seemed to suggest a sense of guilt.

Freud would have said this was the pre-conscious trying to stop the gratification of the wish which was creeping past it in symbolic form.

Jung allowed for the wish, but he then went on to interpret the dream from its finale, and pointed out that the dream was meant to underline the guilt feelings so that the young man should come to terms with the conscience he was trying to ignore, and thus see his behaviour from the view of morality. For Jung the moral attitude did not merely derive from a childhood sense of guilt. He regarded it as archetypal, handed down in the collective unconscious.

Another young man, with homosexual tendencies, had completed his studies yet couldn't decide on a career. He dreamed that he was going up some stairs with his mother and sister. When they reached the top he was told that his sister was pregnant.

For Freud a flight of stairs symbolised sexual intercourse, and the mother and sister had something to do with an incestuous wish.

Jung pointed out rather rationally that if the stairs were to be taken as symbolic, how could the sister, mother, and unborn child be seen as realities. This emphasises one of the problems running through Freudian interpretation – it isn't really scientific if the interpreter can decide which are the symbols and which aren't.

When questioned about his mother, the young man admitted he had not visited her for a long time, and reproached himself for this failure. Jung believed that the mother in the dream in fact represented something that had been neglected, and the young man did agree in some confusion that he had actually neglected his work. When he spoke of his sister he recalled an occasion when he'd kissed her, and understood what the love of a woman could mean. Jung decided that the sister in the dream symbolised 'love for women'. The stairs simply meant growing up and making a success of life. The idea of the child led to the association of becoming a new man.

Jung explained that the dream did not gratify infantile wishes. It was a message from the unconscious to the young man to take up the duties of life he had so far avoided.

The founder of the School of Individual Psychology,

Alfred Adler, regarded the dream as a 'dress-rehearsal for life'. In the dream a person shows his hopes, fears, and plans for the future in symbolic forms, which deal with those aspects the individual cannot bear to face in conscious life. Adler agreed that the dream distorted, not because of some moral censorship relating to infantile desires, but as a protective device for the self in the face of life.

He adhered very much to the dream's compensatory role. People who suffer from an inferiority complex – perhaps due to a physical deformity, or their childhood position within the family – will often be driven by burning ambition in adulthood to compensate for their deficiency and so prove themselves. They may become brilliant artists, statesmen, soldiers . . . or mass-murderers and dictators. According to Adler, people who normally feel they are failures or despised in real life, will frequently dream of being successes, and the centre of attention and adulation.

Wilhelm Stekel saw the dream as 'the signpost which shows the way to the life-conflict'. His technique of interpretation was called 'active psychoanalysis'. It was much quicker than anything suggested by Freud, and depended on *not* allowing the patient to reach a point where he could begin understanding his own dreams. For Stekel this was the time when the analyst should step in and give his own interpretation, rather in the manner of the ancient oneirocritics. In fact, Stekel considered the patient probably tried to deceive the analyst to prevent him understanding the dreams.

Freud believed that Stekel's intuitive interpretation of symbols – mainly related to life, death and sex – damaged the cause of psychoanalysis as much as it helped it Since his use of symbolism is more or less arbitrary, and can be applied mechanically to situations, Stekel's book, also entitled *The Interpretation of Dreams*, has become an important source of material to be developed by later analysts, one of the most famous being Dr Emil Gutheil, an American psychotherapist, who wrote *The Handbook of Dream Analysis*.

For Otto Rank, the pre-natal and birth experiences deeply conditioned the individual's memory. Freud had already put forward the idea that dreams about being buried alive accompanied by a sense of anxiety refer to the unconscious memories of birth, which might have involved respiratory problems and physical constriction.

Birth dreams often depict crawling through dark passages which twist, and never seem to end. There is a feeling of anxiety and difficulty in breathing ... and finally freedom and fresh air. Rank believed that every dream shows the longing to return to the 'pleasurable state' before birth, since it is that experience which caused the first indelible shock ...

For Jung and his followers, the birth dreams point to a person's desire to be re-born, to shake off old habits, to acquire a new life style ... which makes it a forward-looking dream rather than one about a past to which one can never return.

Subsequent analysts have developed further interpretative theories based on one or more of the schools of thought discussed above, and these have been used in the diagnosis and treatment of mental illnesses. Some authorities hold that the kind of interpretation employed should never be rigid, but depend upon the type of analyst and the character of the patient ...

4
The Science of Dreams

So far our examination of dreams and their interpretation has belonged to the infinite realms of art. The two major schools of thought have been followed, developed, and even coordinated by people who saw the benefit in the application of both Jungian and Freudian theories. Yet the process of dreaming remained a matter of speculation. However clever, erudite, or apparently apt, the findings could not be proved.

If science had not begun exploring the whole domain of sleep our knowledge of dreams might well have remained a matter for subjective and intuitive hypothesis.

It had long been thought that the period we spend asleep – although obviously vital to our physical and mental well-being – was a barren area which required man to be unconscious during one third of his life.

Recently, neuro-surgery, precise methods of research, and the invention of sophisticated electrical appliances have enabled the scientists to increase their knowledge of the human brain, the nervous system, and the body's biochemistry.

Despite the great progress already made we still don't know why we sleep or dream, but we are beginning to be aware of much of the detailed mechanics of both processes. In a few years our existing knowledge may well be extended beyond our 'wildest dreams', and by understanding his totality man will learn to control and help himself.

The expression 'I wish I knew what was going on in your mind' is no longer a mere abstraction. The invention of the Electroencephalograph – the EEG – has made it possible for a trained operator to read the brain's reactions during wakefulness, rest and sleep. The machine detects, and enormously amplifies, the very faint electrical impulses produced by the brain by placing electrodes against a subject's scalp. It then transmits them automatically on to graph paper where they appear as an undulating line.

One of the foremost authorities on the whole subject of sleep, Professor Nathanial Kleitman of Chicago University, discovered that babies have a sleep rhythm of between fifty and sixty minutes, after which they are more inclined to wake up, although obviously they don't always.

An analogous situation might be walking across a moorland in thick mist, and finding that at every fifty or sixty yards the mist thinned, but never enough to allow you to be in a clear atmosphere ...

This cycle is not merely a matter of sleeping and

waking, for it can be detected in the EEG tracings, respiration, heartbeat, and blood circulation.

As children grow, they begin to develop the ninety-minute cycle associated with adult sleepers. For people living in our sort of climate, where the hot sun hardly makes taking a siesta a necessary part of the day's events, sleep becomes more or less a single night's stretch.

In other words our pattern of sleep is acquired, and controlled by environmental and social conditioning. As we grow older, however, we tend to revert to the nap-taking habits of babyhood.

Yet, though we more or less choose when we go to sleep, the basic ninety-minute rhythm remains. It is biological, and not controlled by consciousness, rather as a healthy person's metabolism functions autonomously.

In the 1950s, while Kleitman was carrying out some tests on the patterns of sleep and wakefulness in newborn babies, a graduate student, Eugene Aserinsky, noticed that after an infant fell asleep its eyes moved beneath the closed lids . . . also at intervals during sleep . . . and was the first movement when the baby began to wake.

Kleitman and Aserinsky decided to investigate whether such a pattern could be found in adult sleepers. By attaching extra electrodes from the EEG machine to areas around volunteer sleepers' eyes, they were able to monitor brain impulses and eye movements, while measuring respiration and body movements.

Two types of eye movements were recorded: slow as found in babies, and very fast movements which could last from a few minutes to over half an hour. These rapid eye movements – generally known as REMs – appeared to occur at intervals throughout the night.

The EEG tracings showed a definite alteration in brain impulses just before a sleeper began producing these REMs, and at the same time there was an increase in pulse and respiration rates.

By waking the sleepers in an REM phase Kleitman and Aserinsky discovered that REMs were associated with dreaming. This inference was further supported by the fact that people woken during a period without REMs had no dreams to report.

Eyes apparently moved behind their lids because of what they could 'see' happening in a dream. Tests carried out on people who claimed never to dream showed they also produced REMs, which proved, as has always been believed, that everyone dreams – though we don't all possess good memories. From then on, investigators had no need to rely on a subject's recollection of whether or not dreams occurred. The EEG tracings and the REMs were a more reliable guide.

An associate of Professor Kleitman's, Dr Dement, found that the RÉMs and EEG tracings during sleep related to that basic ninety-minute rhythm. The EEG showed four types of sleep, ranging from 'light' to 'deep'.

At the beginning of rest we sink into the deepest sleep, and after eighty to ninety minutes we rise to the lightest kind, and at the same time the REMs begin. Then the process is repeated. During the REMs and light sleep phase breathing is much more rapid, but with the heavy sleep and no REMs respiration becomes slower.

External stimuli, and the need to pass water etc., do not in fact evoke special dreams. Oddly enough, waking someone up during the so-called light sleep when the REMs are taking place can be more difficult than rousing a person from the 'deep' sleep without REMs. Nor does waking someone from 'deep' sleep actually create dreams. When we awake promptly after an REM period, the dream – if we can remember it – of course seems to have happened just before awakening.

There are approximately three REM periods per night, and the intervals dividing them are more or less constant. The later the REMs commence the longer they will last. During these REMs, the EEG records brain wave patterns which resemble those produced when we are awake, so that our consciousness during dreams is far more similar to its waking state than during those non-dreaming periods of sleep.

During our dreams, the brain behaves in many respects as if we are actually awake – the dream images substituting the things we see and experience in waking life. Yet, at the same time, some mechanism prevents us taking physical action by informing our body that these events are only happening in a dream. So long as this mechanism works as it should do, then we act out our fantasies in a cocoon of sleeping safety ... but when it fails to do its job, sleep-talking and somnambulism result. Sleep-walking is an attempt to do something about the dream, and points to some deep problem, so this is a symptom which should always be taken seriously.

The use of the EEG machine demonstrates something that has long been thought to be true – that animals dream ... well, at least some species. Although they can't tell us about their experiences, cats, dogs, sheep, and monkeys all have REM periods during sleep.

Complex experiments by Professor Jouvet of Lyons University have shown that among animals the REM sleep does not stem from the cerebral cortex – the outer layers – but from the primitive areas of the brain. Cats deprived of REM sleep take on a state similar to that found in psychotic human beings, and those suffering from hallucinations.

We all know of the serious psychological disorders which develop in people who have been forcibly deprived of sleep as a subtle method of torture. The discovery of the REM phases allowed Dr Dement to experiment with dream deprivation. Each time the EEG machine produced the brain patterns which heralded an REM area the subject was woken up.

Just as we talk about 'catching up' on our sleep, it appears we have also to 'catch up' on our dreams . . . or rather that we require the sleep for that purpose. When this experiment was carried out over several days more and more REM periods began to occur, until it was impossible to prevent the patient from dreaming except by not allowing him to sleep at all. Naturally, such experiments had to be abandoned, because the patients became undermined and nervous.

However, these tests do suggest that we *need* to dream so much that in order to fulfil this necessity all the basic patterns for sleep and waking can be broken by whatever the mechanism is that produces our dreams.

Without dreams we might even die. Cats, who were prevented from having any REM sleep over a long period, as part of Professor Jouvet's tests, died without there being any other apparent cause. So people who have suffered from sleep deprivation may, in fact, derive their mental disturbances, such as hallucinations, from dream deprivation.

As yet inconclusive, but still immensely intriguing, are another set of elaborate experiments which have recently been conducted in America. They have demonstrated that in the male the periods of penile erection, which occur during the night, begin at the same time as the commencement of the REMs, and persist throughout this phase.

For many years, a fact that has been widely accepted, but which remains uncorroborated by science, is that women's dreams are in some way stimulated by their menstrual cycle. Many women claim that for some nights prior to the onset of menstruation, dreaming seems to become particularly intense.

Of course, by discussing these ideas we seem to be harking back to Freud. Yet, such theories do suggest a much vaster concept of sexuality, which would appear to be connected in some way with the body's biochemical processes, rather than any thwarted infantile sexual desire ...

So far, no way has been discovered of checking on what any person is dreaming about except by waking him or her after a recorded REM period. Dr Dement suggests that the direction of the eye movements, as recorded by the EEG machine, corresponds with what the eye is actually seeing in the dream. Experiments, which involved waking the dreamer, and checking his account of a dream with the patterns traced by the EEG machine, have in some instances attested to this theory.

A woman, who dreamed she walked up some stairs, produced tracings showing a pronounced upward direction. Someone who dreamed of a fight which involved two men throwing tomatoes at each other produced eye movements rather like those you see in the crowd watching the activities on the Wimbledon centre court.

Tests on subjects who were born blind show no REMs, a fact which is confirmed by the dreamers' reports. These unsighted people's dreams do not contain visual images, since they have no sighted memories as a foundation. Apparently they dream in terms of touch, since this is how they experience their surroundings during consciousness.

Anyway not everyone depends completely on pictorial matter in their dreams. Some are more aware of dream sounds . . . others of odours. One woman claimed she could often smell a corpse. Analysis showed this related to a traumatic incident concerning death during her childhood. Other people seem to dream in words or phrases, and wake up with what they think are significant sentences. When these are repeated aloud they frequently make no particular sense, or don't convey the feelings of profound knowledge that they did in the dream. Once again careful analysis may reveal just what these words are pointing towards.

Despite the progress made in experimental techniques, it is still very tricky to carry out tests on sleepers, and so arrive at any concrete conclusion regarding the nature and contents of dreams. Do the very techniques of the sleep laboratories alter or affect the type of dreams? Time and further research may well soon solve this problem.

However, it seems more than a vague suggestion to state that there is often a relationship between the several dreams which occur during one night. They may contain totally dissimilar episodes, but on closer examination these may reveal that they are in fact linked by a basic theme or emotion . . . rather as if several people were each asked to make a short film about some strong feeling: grief, anger, frustration. Of course, the films would be different, but they would still bear some relationship to each other ...

Clearly, the reporting of our dreams – even in the strictly regulated atmosphere of the sleep laboratory – is entirely dependent on memory ... and this, as we know, may be totally, or partially unreliable.

Why do we forget these dreams? For most of them are simply not remembered, while those vaguely recalled on waking will disappear unless they're written down or related to somebody else. A subject woken just after an REM phase, which may have lasted for thirty minutes, will not be able to recall any more than if he'd just had a short dream.

This is the reason why, in psychotherapy, there is no point in attempting to take what the patient relates about a dream as anything more than mere snatches, which may even have appeared in a different order during dreaming. So often what is recalled might be the work of the conscious mind trying to turn blurred memories of the dream into a neat anecdote.

Therefore, analysts who employ dream therapy must always be aware that the patient unconsciously chooses the dream contents to relate. This, of course, doesn't negate the use of such therapy. For, by his choice, a patient is unwittingly revealing his psychological make-up.

The examples of Maury's dreams described in the first section of this book suggested that they must have all happened in a flash, because they were based upon what he remembered immediately on waking. Now that we know dreaming takes place at intervals throughout sleep this premise would appear to be false.

Obviously sometimes the action in a dream may seem to take a very long time indeed. It can cover such a wide variety of incidents, full of details and entailing complex emotions, that it would appear to be impossible for them all to be squeezed into the span of one night. How can such a procedure take place, even in the longest REM phase?

Daily life can illustrate this possibility quite clearly. ... You're standing in a bus queue, watching the people around. Just from snatches of conversation, appearances, or behaviour you infer all sorts of complicated conclusions about their lives, emotions, jobs, and relationships. You are not making up a piece of fiction though: it is merely that quite complex details of other people's lives and situations become apparent during a very short, and not particularly intensive, period of observation.

All this time, naturally, you are perhaps studying the headlines in someone else's evening paper, and are aware of the weather ... almost subliminally you notice the shops, the buildings, a dog, perhaps you like or dislike some item in a shop window; remember what you have to do at work in the morning, something you have left undone at home ... and maybe that evening's special date. Then, the bus arrives. You may have only been waiting a few minutes. If you're late, upset, in a hurry, or it's cold, it might *feel* like hours . . . and during that time various highly involved ideas have been running through your mind at several levels, probably involving memories from long ago, and also hopes and plans for the future . . .

The medium of the cinema presents another useful analogy. A particular sequence may take no longer than ten minutes. In that time you have witnessed a series of events which would have taken hours, days, or even years to happen in real life, yet it seems quite convincing while you watch the screen.

If asked to describe one of the scenes, you'd probably give a fairly sweeping account: '. . . two men were sitting at a table in a pavement cafe in Paris. They discussed how to steal some famous diamonds from a millionaire in the Bahamas . . .'

Required to relate more about the scene, you'd begin to recall all sorts of minute details, which you'd noticed without being really aware of them: '. . . the sun was shining . . . the chestnut trees in bloom . . . one man smoked a pipe . . . they both drank pernod . . . the girl at the next table was reading *Elle* . . . she was wearing a maxi dress like the one you saw in a shop . . . and a yellow hat . . .' etc., etc. All these factors have been incorporated into the scene, not because they're vital to the plot, but to give depth and feeling. You accept them without question, for due to them the action on the screen seems very real, but most of your mind is actually concentrating on the unrolling of the story.

In the film it takes a few minutes for the hero to leave London and fly to the Bahamas. This might be depicted by a scene at London Airport . . . it is raining . . . the hero wears a raincoat. The huge plane takes off . . . then there's glorious sunshine. Our hero, tanned and in bathing trunks, strolls along a fabulous beach in the company of some bikini-clad beauty. Although we know it would take hours for all this to happen in reality we accept the scenes completely.

This now seems to be the likely explanation for what happens in dreams . . . and why on recall they often seem so bizarre is because we can only remember fragments; and put together they don't make sense. Certainly, Freudian free-association is a useful aid to finding the emotional connections between images.

From the development of techniques described, used in conjunction with drugs, hypnosis, and external stimuli, much essential data about dreaming is being collected. The controlled use of hallucinogenic substances, like LSD 25, is enabling the scientists to send subjects into a state very similar to one of dreaming, without divesting them of consciousness, so that they can describe exactly what is taking place as it happens.

The more we begin to know, the more there appears to be to discover. Although dreams are still a mystery, it seems we are on a definite track towards solving and unravelling one of the most intriguing secrets of mankind.

At the same time we must realise that the scientific research being carried out, which has brought about these discoveries of the biochemical processes attached to dreaming, in no way eradicates the theories of Freud and Jung. What it does do is to enlarge upon them, making the horizon wider and more exciting, and showing that dreams are a physical and psychological necessity.

Another so far inconclusive fact about dreaming is that some people claim to dream in colour, but most say they dream in black and white with occasional touches of colour. One authority on dreams insists that everyone dreams in colour, only they don't recall doing so. Other theories are that the colours in our dreams alter as we develop our personalities and mature. One modern French writer suggests that dreams in colour spring from a deeper area of the unconscious than the black and white ones ...

In the same decade that the existence of the REM cycle was discovered, Russian doctors were attempting to test the ancient theory of 'prodromic' dreams – that a dream could give advance warning of some sickness before there were any physical signs.

Certainly some patients admitted to very curious dreams before they were actually found to be ill. Prior to tuberculosis being diagnosed, a girl student regularly dreamed of being buried alive. She could even feel the cold heaviness of the damp earth pressing on her body, and woke sweating with fear.

For several weeks before other patients had their illnesses diagnosed, they dreamed of knives cutting into their insides, and being knocked on the head. People, who were operated upon for cerebral tumours, reported that a year or so before any symptom of the disease appeared they had dreams in which they were wounded in the head ... invariably in the identical spot as the tumour.

Although we have to admit that such findings are very strange indeed, and sound almost incontestable, these 'prodromic' dreams cannot safely be used for discovering sickness because many people, who are perfectly healthy, experience similar types of dreams...

So far, we have only considered the dreams of adults, but since this process appears to be instinctual we can increase the depth of our knowledge about dreaming by looking at the details available on children's dreams.

Research has demonstrated that new-born babies have REM cycles which in adults signify the occurrance of a dream. Therefore we can infer that a baby dreams long before we would imagine it had anything to dream about. This gives another boost to the suggestion that the dream periods are a basic biological function. Obviously, until some scientific method is devised by which we can know exactly what is going on in the mind of a creature unable to speak, our supposition on what babies dream of remains purely speculative.

One ingenious theory put forward was that babies dreamed everything new they saw and experienced as if they were digesting each day's fresh supply of material, which was why they needed so much sleep...

Freud's example of Hermann and the basket of cherries probably gives a clear sample of the sort of thing most small children dream about. Obviously the earlier an infant learns to talk the quicker do we gain an idea of the contents of its dreams.

During their second year children definitely do dream, and there appears to be evidence that trains figure frequently in these dreams.

At three children may report the occasional dream. From such samples it seems the contents are about everyday things: parents, playing, and farm animals. At around $3\frac{1}{2}$ dreams may cause tears.

Four-year-olds seem to dream of parents, friends, games, and sometimes the flapping of birds' wings. Another half year produces a lot of animal dreams, especially about wolves.

Five is the age of nightmares, which disturb and terrify, and the children are often unable to recount these dreams. Samples suggest that there is a predominance of *bad* animals, like wolves and bears, which chase the child. Strange or *bad* people of weird colouring and appearance also play a part. Fire, water, fighting, and punishment are other features. It is at this age that the child may confuse dreams and waking imagination.

It's a relief to learn that at $5\frac{1}{2}$ children's dreams begin to be less distressing. There are still wolves, bears, and snakes, which fight, bite and threaten to hurt the child – and his dog, if there is one – but by now the child can report these bad dreams. Another aspect of them is that 'things' are in the bed. Some children talk in their sleep, and of course there are also pleasant everyday dreams.

The six-year-old has dreams of something having happened to Mother, and impersonal problems begin to appear: war, fire and thunder. *Bad* people and animals still occur, and there are 'things' in the bedroom, but laughter during the child's sleep suggests there are also plenty of enjoyable dreams.

Seven is another time for nightmares. Being chased, or threatened, and rooted to the spot are quite common dreams. Burglars, war, and ghosts also appear. At this time there are lots of water dreams – swimming, boating, drowning – and also dreams of flying and floating. In all these fantasies the child plays the central role, and at this age – if it hasn't already happened – television and films have an influence on the dream contents.

Children of eight and nine enjoy their dreams, and like to tell them. Often they don't want to be woken up during dreaming, and will try to go back to sleep and finish off the dreams. Now, pleasant contents abound, and nightmares are rare. Dreams can be about personal problems, possessions, and friends. Mystery stories will influence the contents.

Nightmares again predominate with ten-year-olds. There are dragons, robbers, *bad* men, the fear of being chased and murdered. The child may cry out without waking...

Gradually with the onset of teenage pleasant dreams begin to overtake nightmares, and dreaming starts to become comparable with adult styles. Often at puberty a young person will experience those significant dreams about which Jung wrote. These deal with some religious or important abstract matter, and seem to signify that the unconscious is seeking out the individual's road to development.

Even though our sleeping time diminishes as we grow up, REMs take up 18.5 per cent of it until after eighteen years of age. Then they rise to account for about one quarter of the time. This amount slowly decreases with old age.

We have mentioned the nightmare in connection with children's dreams, but of course it also affects adults. This far from enjoyable experience is a frequent reason for people being unable to sleep. The fear that they will once again encounter those really ghastly dreams keeps both shell-shocked soldiers, civilians, and little children awake. For the effects of the nightmare don't end with morning light. They persist throughout the day.

The predominant feature in childhood nightmares is the appearance of some kind of monster: a witch, a vampire, a werewolf. The word 'nightmare' originally meant an incubus or monster. According to Ernest Jones, Freud's biographer, and a follower of Freudian theories, these monsters represent the parents, and the nightmare is to do with infantile sexuality – 'an expression of mental conflict over an incestuous desire'. In many cases sexual fears may be the correct interpretation of those 'bad' dreams, but of course we have other instinctive terrors ... especially of being smothered.

In his book *Dreams and Nightmares* J. A. Hadfield divides nightmares into three types:

1. Those which spring from some particular childhood or adult experience. Quite common sources of nightmares are the experience of birth, or an early operation, or some other unpleasant treatment for a childhood illness, or the threat by an adult that 'something will get you if you're not good'. Anyone who has known the horrific experiences which accompany all warfare will at times re-live them in his dreams.

2. 'Nightmares resulting from the fear of our own impulses': those instances when our most primitive instincts – terror, anger, or sex – seem to be about to overcome us and gain control. The emotions reappear in nightmares represented by symbols or people.

Hadfield cites an example of a dream which demonstrates this fear of being overwhelmed. A girl had a nightmare in which some horrible creatures were pursuing her to carry her off, and make her one of themselves. The girl felt herself being threatened by her emotions which she had transformed into 'horrible creatures' and she feared being turned into one of these monsters...

3. 'Nightmares which are objectifications of our organic sensations': crabs, vampires, and spiders are a feature of these. Although Jung saw such creatures as arche-

types, Hadfield regarded them as symbolising certain universal basic feelings.

Originally such feelings frighten the tiny child, and remain in its memory as sensations which could over-power it. Pain and discomfort in the tummy may make a child feel as if some horrid crab is clawing at his vitals.

Children, animals, and primitive minds can't help locating the blame outside themselves, as if some un-seen being is causing their troubles. It is not 'I have a nasty pain'. Rather it is, 'this nasty pain isn't my doing', thus transforming the 'it' into a vile creature which is 'doing this bad thing to me'.

In much the same way the child's experience of orgasm, that leaves it feeling weak and overpowered, becomes the vampire which has drawn off all its strength. These fears, of course, are often increased by parental rebukes and warnings.

Since the fact of dreaming is now recognised as an integral part of human existence, it is some relief to realise that our deepest terrors, as they appear in dreams, are shared by other individuals. We are not alone: and even at our most seemingly isolated moments our mental and physical conditions relate us to mankind past and present, and probably of the far-flung future . . .

5
Dreams and Dreamers

MORE 'TYPICAL' DREAMS

THERE are certain significant dreams that ancient and modern dream books, and analysts, tell us occur in the dream life of most individuals ... naturally differing in details but always with the same basic subjects. We have seen how Freud interpreted some of these. Now, let us look at other 'typical' dreams, and their various meanings.

Missing a Train. 'I ran along an endless platform forever bumping into people ... but the train started to move ... I ran harder but I couldn't catch it. Everything seemed set to prevent me ...'

For Freud the dreams that depict the departure of a train you have failed to catch are all about death. The train symbolises death. The failure to board it expresses the dreamer's unconscious desire to comfort himself that he isn't about to die.

However, it has been pointed out that in a dream

when we manage to catch the train we experience a sense of relief and satisfaction ... whereas missing it invariably produces anxiety or frustration. Another interpretation explains that this train journey actually represents the progress through life, and so missing it indicates a fear that we are not advancing as we should wish ... or that we need to alter our attitudes in order to develop.

Climbing. 'I dreamed I climbed up very high, and felt great happiness when I reached the top ...'

Dreams of mounting, or descending stairs, ladders, mountains, or similar, were interpreted by Freud as signifying penile erection and orgasm ... or detumescence after orgasm. This isn't an exactly satisfactory explanation for female dreamers though. Other interpretations are that the dream reveals the desire to achieve our ambitions, to reach the top of our chosen profession, or to be promoted in some way ...

Falling. 'I was drifting off to sleep ... in fact I might have been asleep ... when suddenly I felt myself falling ... falling. I woke abruptly ...'

This weird sensation in a dream is often associated with the fall in blood pressure which accompanies the beginning of sleep. It may be, however, the remains of some primordial fear from the days when our ancestors lived in trees, and falling must have been a dangerous hazard. Of course, the feeling is also related to a memory of orgasm.

Some authorities suggest that falling dreams symbolise the fear of a moral lapse, which especially worries women. It can also be an anxiety about failure, and being toppled from some proud and elevated position. Other memories that might inspire this dream are from early childhood, when we always seemed to be tumbling over, and a fear that we might return to that period in life when we had no rights or control over ourselves . . .

Flying or Floating. We know that Freud explained this kind of dream as being connected with infantile sexual sensations. Others interpret it as a memory of the pre-birth existence. Some see it, of course, as an archaic echo from the time when our aquatic ancestry floated in a vast sea. Some authorities see flying dreams as the wish to overcome the difficulties in life . . . or the method by which the unconscious compensates the individual for those waking feelings of inferiority. It may also symbolise the longing to escape from a particular situation, or life pattern . . .

Swimming. 'I dreamed I was swimming in a great lake, struggling against the current. The beach seemed so far away I believed I could never reach it . . .'

For Freud this was the sexual desire to return to the mother's womb. Other authorities cite the memory of birth, or of an actual childhood experience – perhaps of swimming, and suddenly finding you're out of your depth, and that the tide is trying to drag you further from the shore – or, again, it could be one of those archaic memories. Other interpretations are that swimming dreams symbolise the dreamer's struggle with his basic impulses, or that the unconscious is attempting to encourage the dreamer to fight on to attain his particular goal in waking life.

Falling Teeth. This is a very strange and sometimes frightening dream. Freud considered it symbolised the emission of semen, or the fear of castration, and he wrote that Jung believed this dream was about bearing children. Another interpretation is that the dream signifies 'growing-up' – based on the memory of milk teeth falling, at an important stage of childhood development.

Death of the Dreamer. An individual's dream of his own death, or funeral, may symbolise the unconscious yearning to return to the security of the maternal womb or the desire for a fresh birth, a new life, resurrection . . .

Nudity. Freud's explanation of this is dealt with earlier in the book, but all other theories about being naked and anxious in a dream give the release of repressed longings as its inspiration. An interpretation could be that the dreamer longs to show his, or her, true self to the world, but fears criticism and disapproval . . .

Crime and Punishment. A dream of committing some

crime is interpreted as the wish, or thought, that the conscious mind has rejected . . . like the infantile desire for a parent's death. If this forbidden longing is satisfied in a dream – even in a very distorted form – the unconscious often attempts to balance it with a dream of punishment, which will atone for the wish, and arises from the basic sense of guilt.

Being Chased and Rooted to the Spot. This can often be more of a nightmare than a dream. In women, dreams of being chased can symbolise the longing to be wooed. The word 'chased' could even be a pun on 'chaste', for sometimes a woman's wish to be courted can be accompanied by a desire not to lose her virginity. Another interpretation is that the dream is about sexual intercourse culminating in orgasm . . . either the longing for or the fear of the act. It might also arise out of those fears in childhood when we want to flee from something frightening, and find we haven't the physical power to do so.

The literature of dreams, and their interpretations, is extensive and fascinating. It starts with the earliest poem known, the Assyrian *Epic of Gilgamesh*, and is a feature of Homeric tales. It is hard to think of Shakespeare's plays without recalling some famous dream scene: *Macbeth*, *A Midsummer Night's Dream*, *Richard III*, *Romeo and Juliet*.

The artist has always used the dream motif to introduce fantasy, allegory, symbolism, messages from the gods and the dead, and to herald the future. No doubt the device will endure until the last dream is dreamed, or the final tale told ...

FAMOUS DREAMERS AND THEIR DREAMS

Not all dreams end with waking. Sometimes it seems that their contents reflect or inspire future events with a clarity which requires no special method of interpretation. Dreaming has conveyed the answer to problems, the foreknowledge of certain death. It has allowed the muse to whisper the seeds of some idea into the sleeping composer, writer, or philosopher. One other phenomenon, never satisfactorily explained, is the predictive, warning dream which is horrifically mirrored by a subsequent actual happening ...

The Dream as Muse

When he was about twenty-one the Italian composer, Guiseppe Tartini, worked on a sonata which he seemed unable to complete. One night he had a dream in which he sold his soul to the devil. He gave the devil his violin to see what he would do with it, and was astonished to hear him play an exquisite sonata. 'I was delighted, transported, enchanted, I was breathless and I woke up. Seizing my violin, I tried to reproduce the sounds I had heard. But in vain. The piece I composed, the 'Devil's Trill', was the best I have ever written, but how remote it was from the one I had heard in my dream!'

Robert Louis Stevenson made a point of remembering and using his dreams as a fertile source of material. He suffered from tuberculosis, and there is a suggestion that the disease may well have kept his sleep at the 'light' stage, which we now know is associated with REMs, and therefore his percentage of dreaming time might have been greater than usual.

In childhood, Stevenson's dreams tended towards the nightmarish variety. Later they contained journeys and scenery. Then, he began to dream whole stories, and each night was able to continue dreaming where he'd left off the previous morning. This experience became so horrifying that he was forced to seek medical advice.

He actually dreamed the idea for the transformation of one character into another, on which the story for *Dr Jekyll and Mr Hyde* was based, and he incorporated into it his own experiences of a dual existence from alternating between dream life and real life.

Dr Jekyll and Mr Hyde is an apt example of Freud's theory that man, who at the conscious level is decent, respectable, and civilised, contains an uncontrolled other half – the unconscious – which is a mass of primitive urges always trying to get loose. There again, *Dr Jekyll* might serve as an equally useful example of Jung's concept of the persona, while *Mr Hyde* is the shadow which houses all his least admirable aspects.

When Stevenson started to create stories commercially, he employed his dreams as sources and critics of the material. He called these muses the 'little people', and believed that they showed him in their theatre either a complete play, or else a series of instalments. For Stevenson the dreams were the real authors, and his conscious self merely did the practical work . . . writing down what the 'little people' had shown him, preparing the material, and selling it.

The poet, Samuel Taylor Coleridge, was an opium-eater, but the drug did not give him his brilliant technique, the vast store of memories from reading, nor the flame of inspiration.

However, it was through an opium dream that the unfinished poem *Kubla Khan* came into existence. Coleridge's own account of the occasion admitted that he'd taken a dose of laudanum for some indisposition. He fell asleep for about three hours while reading from Purcha's *His Pilgrimage*. The passage he read was probably this one:

In Xamdu did Cublai Can build a stately palace, encompassing sixteene miles of plaine ground with a wall wherein are fertile Meddowes, pleasant springs, delightful Streames, and all sorts of beasts of chase and game, and in the middest thereof a sumptuous house of pleasure, which may be removed from place to place . . .

During the time he slept, Coleridge dreamed that he'd composed between two and three hundred lines of poetry, and then awoke, clearly remembering all of it. Instantly he began to write *Kubla Khan* . . .

In Xanadu did Kubla Khan
A stately pleasure-dome decree:
Where Alph, the sacred river, ran
Through caverns measureless to man
Down to a sunless sea.
So twice five miles of fertile ground
With walls and towers were girdled round:
And there were gardens bright with sinuous rills
Where blossom'd many an incense-bearing tree;
And here were forests ancient as the hills,
Enfolding sunny spots of greenery ...

Coleridge had put down fifty-four lines, when he was interrupted by 'a person on business from Porlock'. An hour later, when he was able to return to this poem, he discovered that the memory of his dream had fled, leaving him only eight or ten odd lines.

If Coleridge had been able to capture his whole dream on paper undoubtedly that poem would have continued as magnificently as it had begun. Many people, who read and travel, must have a store of wonderful images in their unconscious, but how few are they who have dreams which synthesise the fragments into such artistry.

The Dream as a Solution

Certainly that hackneyed piece of advice 'why not sleep on it?', offered when you have a problem to solve, sounds less ridiculous when we see how dreaming has helped various experts. Where an answer to some scientific or philosophical problem reveals itself in a dream, the authorities tell us that this is because all the factors for such an answer are present within the sleeper's knowledge. It is just a matter of permutating them correctly. The only consolation available for most of us, who do not have these useful dreams, is that perhaps we don't possess all the necessary data...

The French philosopher, Condorcet, used to leave incomplete difficult calculations, and then go to sleep. Frequently, the answers appeared in his dreams...

For years, the German chemist, F. A. Kekulé, had been seeking for what is now known as the benzene ring which revolutionised organic chemistry. While writing his chemical text book, he fell into a doze. Afterwards he described the dream: 'I turned the chair to the fireplace and sank into a half sleep. The atoms flitted before my eyes . . . wriggling and turning like snakes . . . one of the snakes seized its own tail, and the image whirled scornfully before my eyes. As though from a flash of lightning I awoke. I occupied the rest of the night in working out the consequences of the hypothesis...' and he encouraged his listeners with 'Let us learn to dream, gentlemen...'

Once again the unconscious processes of the dream had solved a problem in terms of the symbolism so often used in dreaming.

Dr Hilprecht, a professor at Pennsylvania University in the 1890s, tried to read the cuneiform characters on two small pieces of agate, which were believed to be Babylonian rings belonging to the reign of King

Kurigalzu, who lived around 1300 BC. The professor could not decide what these rings actually were.

One night, in a long dream, a Babylonian priest appeared and took him to a treasure room, where he told Hilprecht that the fragments were pieces of a votive cylinder cut into three to make earrings for a statue of the god Ninib.

When he awoke, the professor once more examined the objects, and found the parts in fact fitted together ... and that the inscription contained the names of Kurigalzu and Ninib...

Another dream which solved a problem, this time of a financial nature, is said to have happened in the 15th century to a pedlar named John Chapman, from Swaffham in Suffolk. This apparently true tale really seems to belong with 'Dick Whittington' and 'Aladdin'...

Chapman dreamed he had to go to London, and that on London Bridge he would meet with a stranger who would tell him of a fortune. He followed up this dream, and went to London. On London Bridge he did meet a man, who in turn told him that he had dreamed about a Swaffham pedlar who had money buried in his garden.

John Chapman hurried home ... to dig up the money!

Carvings on a Suffolk Church which Chapman had built with part of his 'dream' money testify to this extraordinary story ...

Dreams that Foretell the Dreamer's Death

Those images which predict the death of the dreamer, or a close relative, are among the most frequent examples of the prophetic dream.

Naturally, if someone close to you is very ill, you may well dream of their death. If this does occur, the dream must seem more than pure coincidence. We can't yet know if people who dream correctly of their own imminent death have some unconscious knowledge that they are mortally sick, although this seems the most likely explanation.

None of us can any longer be astonished that famous men – especially in the light of so many recent tragedies – must constantly be aware that they are risking assassination.

A dream of a rainbow above the head of the dreamer used to be interpreted by some as an omen of a violent death. The night before he was assassinated in 1610 by Ravaillac, Henry IV, King of France, had such a dream ...

A few days before he was murdered, Abraham Lincoln described a dream in which he was wandering through the White House. Suddenly he came upon a crowd of mourners, and a military guard surrounding a catafalque on which rested a coffin. When he asked the identity of the dead person, he was told that the president had been killed by an assassin ...

Champmeslé was a French actor who died in 1701.

Two days before his own death, he dreamed that his dead wife and mother appeared, and that the latter beckoned him to follow them.

The actor repeated the contents of this dream to his friends, and actually paid for his own funeral mass to be sung. As he was leaving the church he began talking to some acquaintances, and dropped down dead...

Prophetic Dreams

On the night before President John F. Kennedy's assassination, a woman is said to have phoned the White House, and claimed that she had dreamed that the president would be killed in Dallas, Texas...

Yet, can we really pay attention to such dreams? After all, whenever there's a lot of publicity because someone or something has disappeared, countless people always come forward with accounts of their dreams, which tell where to locate the missing person or object. There is no reason to doubt that they did dream, but the results rarely prove successful.

When we consider what a personal matter the process of dreaming is, it seems highly unlikely that any individual can dream of something which is not already within their own unconscious mind . . . or at least closely bound up with their life and emotions.

Yet, there have been indisputable accounts of personal dreams, which relate to much wider issues. Sometimes though, as in the case of one of Napoleon's dreams, the situation has reached a point where it is far too late, or utterly impossible, to heed the warning contained in the dream. The night before the Battle of Waterloo, Napoleon had two dreams in which he saw a black cat cross from one army to the other, and his own army being cut to pieces.

The danger of interpreting dreams in purely sexual terms is neatly demonstrated in the account of Bismarck's famous dream about the Austrian war. Freud explained this was really about infantile masturbation. Jung interpreted it as a dream which impelled Bismarck towards success by showing him that success. In a letter to the Emperor William I, Bismarck described his dream:

Your Majesty's communication encourages me to relate a dream which I had in the spring of 1863, in the worst days of the struggle, from which no human eye could see any possible escape. I dreamt (as I related the first thing next morning to my wife and other witnesses) that I was riding on a narrow Alpine path, precipice on the right, rocks on the left. The path grew narrower, so that the horse refused to proceed, and it was impossible to turn round or dismount, owing to lack of space. Then, with my whip in my left hand, I struck the smooth rock and called on God. The whip grew to an endless length, the rocky wall dropped like a piece of stage scenery and opened out a broad path, with a view over hills and forests, like a landscape in Bohemia; there were Prussian troops with banners, and even in my dream the thought came to me at once that I must report it to your Majesty. This dream was fulfilled, and I woke up rejoiced and strengthened ...

It has been said that the evidence collected about hundreds of prophetic and telepathic dreams still doesn't solve the mystery whether or not a prediction which comes true is a psychic phenomenon, or merely one of those million-to-one coincidences. Some authorities suggest that there is no such thing as 'time' as we understand it, and that sometimes individuals are empowered to glimpse the past, the future, or somewhere a great distance away.

J. W. Dunne described a dream he had in the autumn of 1913 in his book, *An Experiment with Time*. In this dream he saw that a train had fallen over the embankment to the north of the Firth of Forth Bridge. He had a feeling that such an accident would take place the following spring.

He related this dream to his sister, and both of them, without any real conviction, went on to warn their friends against travelling north in the spring.

On April 14, 1914, the Flying Scotsman was derailed. It crashed down an embankment north of the Forth Bridge ...

We can't know if the avoidance of a single incident could prevent a world-shattering catastrophe. However, there have been two dreams which might have altered recent world history: the first by being heeded, the second if it had been ignored ...

In June 1914, Bishop Joseph Lanyi, tutor to the Archduke Franz Ferdinand, had a dream that the Archduke would be assassinated at Sarajevo. Not only did the bishop try to warn Franz Ferdinand, he wrote down the incident, and drew a sketch of it. When Lanyi failed to make himself believed, he celebrated a mass for the Archduke early in the morning.

On June 28, the dream came true. It was the spark which ignited the holocaust known as the First World War ...

The edition of the French magazine, *Match*, which appeared on September 22, 1938, gave an account of Adolf Hitler's dream which took place in 1917. At that time, he was a corporal in the Bavarian Infantry on the French front.

He dreamed of being buried under a great mound of earth and molten iron, and could feel the warmth of blood spilling down his chest. The dream woke him abruptly.

The area of the Somme that the Bavarian troops were defending seemed very quiet, but Hitler still felt anxious and restless. He left the trench and wandered towards the open country, telling himself that he was being stupid because there was certainly more danger outside the trench from shrapnel or a bullet.

But the impact of his dream seemed to hold him prisoner, and he could only go on walking. At a burst of gunfire, Hitler threw himself on to the ground. The dream and its effects forgotten, he rushed back to the trench.... It had disappeared completely, and all his comrades were buried alive.

From that day onwards, Hitler claimed to have become convinced that he had been entrusted with some divine mission ...

We have only been able to take a broad look at what has been believed and discovered about dreaming ... its processes, nature, and interpretation. Although we are still free to choose what we think the dream means, and where it comes from, one thing is absolutely clear, that our sleeping visions can never be dismissed as:

> ... children of an idle brain
> Begot of nothing, but vain fantasy ...

Further Reading

R. de Becker, *The Understanding of Dreams – or The Machinations of the Night*, Allen & Unwin, 1968

G. Dudley, *Dreams: Their Mysteries Revealed*, The Aquarian Press, 1969

Havelock Ellis, *The World of Dreams*, London, 1911

S. Freud, *The Interpretation of Dreams*, Allen & Unwin, 1954
   On Dreams, Hogarth, 1952

J. A. Hadfield, *Dreams and Nightmares*, Penguin, 1969

E. Harms (Ed.), *Problems of Sleep and Dream in Children*, Pergamon, 1964

C. Jung, *Integration of the Personality*, Routledge, 1948
   Modern Man in Search of a Soul, Routledge, 1933
   Two Essays on Analytical Psychology, Routledge, 1953

N. Kleitman, *Sleep and Wakefulness*, University of Chicago Press, 1963

J. Layard, *The Lady of the Hare, a Study in the Healing Power of Dreams*, Faber and Faber, 1944

N. Mackenzie, *Dreams and Dreaming*, Aldus, 1965

R. Robbins, *The Encyclopedia of Witchcraft and Demonology*, Paul Hamlyn, 1959

J. M. Scott, *The White Poppy – The History of Opium*, Heinemann, 1969

W. Stekel, *The Interpretation of Dreams*, Liveright, 1943

ABOUT THE AUTHOR

Sandra Shulman is a Londoner and a full-time writer. After college, she wrote children's stories while working in Hulton Press fiction department. She has travelled extensively gathering facts, especially in areas with occult connections, and her particular interests are European history and comparative religion. She has published seven novels, two of which – *The Daughters of Satan* and *The Degenerates* – have the theme of witchcraft. She lives in London.

ACKNOWLEDGMENTS

We are grateful to the following for permission to use copyright prints and photographs:

Foto Leif Geiges, 8; Sonia Halliday Photographs, 6; Mansell Collection, 1; Picturepoint London, 5, 7; Radio Times Hulton Picture Library, 2, 3, 9.

Close Ups of the High Sierra

CLOSE UPS

of the

by

Norman Clyde

LA SIESTA PRESS

HIGH SIERRA

revised edition

ILLUSTRATED BY

Ruth Daly

EDITED BY

Walt Wheelock

Glendale, Calif.   1976

A climbing manual is not a substitute for climbing practice or skill. Proper equipment will tend to make rockclimbs safer, but only if safety policies are always practiced. It is urged that inexperienced mountaineers will avail themselves of the instruction and guidance that the climbing groups of our various mountaineering clubs are so willing to supply to serious students of the climbing arts.

LA SIESTA PRESS

Box 406
Glendale, California, 91209

PRINTED IN U. S. A.

Contents

Preface

HERE IS presented the first collection of the mountaineering writings of Norman Clyde. While he is best known for his fabulous ascents in the High Sierra, Glacier Park and elsewhere, he was a very prolific writer on alpine matters for a decade and a half from 1927 to 1942. He contributed over three dozen articles to TOURING TOPICS and its successor, WESTWAYS, during this period. His works appeared regularly in the SIERRA CLUB BULLETIN and other mountaineering journals. Unfortunately none of his articles has been available in book form and it is felt that this publication will fill a real need in the field of mountaineering writing.

The main body of the text is given over to a series of five articles, which even today far surpass any other "Close Ups of our High Sierra" that have since been published. Included also are two stories of first ascents that Clyde made, a listing of his known (undoubtedly the unrecorded list is also long) first ascents, and a listing of his writings in magazines of California.

We are most grateful to Norman Clyde for allowing the republication of these stories and for his assistance in the preparation of the material. His journals and photographic file were placed at our disposal and he spent long hours in reviewing and discussing his life and work in the High Sierra.

We are also grateful to Patrice Manahan of WESTWAYS, Dorothy Cutler of the SOUTHERN SIERRAN and, David R. Brower of the SIERRA CLUB BULLETIN for consenting to the use of articles first appearing in these magazines.

W. W.

Norman Clyde 1885-1972
SUMMIT Magazine photo

"Close Ups" of Our High Sierra

Climbing guides to the Sierra Nevada were slow to develop. Clarence King's MOUNTAINEERING IN THE SIERRA NEVADA, which was first published in 1872, was much more a series of adventure stories than any sort of a guide. While Le Conte, Solomons and Farquhar had published articles in the Sierra Club Bulletin, nothing in the nature of a guide in book form was to be published until the Sierra Club brought out its A CLIMBER'S GUIDE TO THE HIGH SIERRA in 1956.

So it is little wonder that Norman Clyde's authoritive series of articles, "CLOSE-UPS" OF OUR HIGH SIERRA" was eagerly received when they appeared in Touring Topics in 1928. The copies quickly became collector's items as they disappeared into the libraries of Sierra peak baggers. They are here reprinted as Clyde wrote them, even to the elevations that were then accepted. (Current elevations are listed in the Index.)

Darwin Ridge from Lake Sabrina
Photo by Walt Wheelock

9

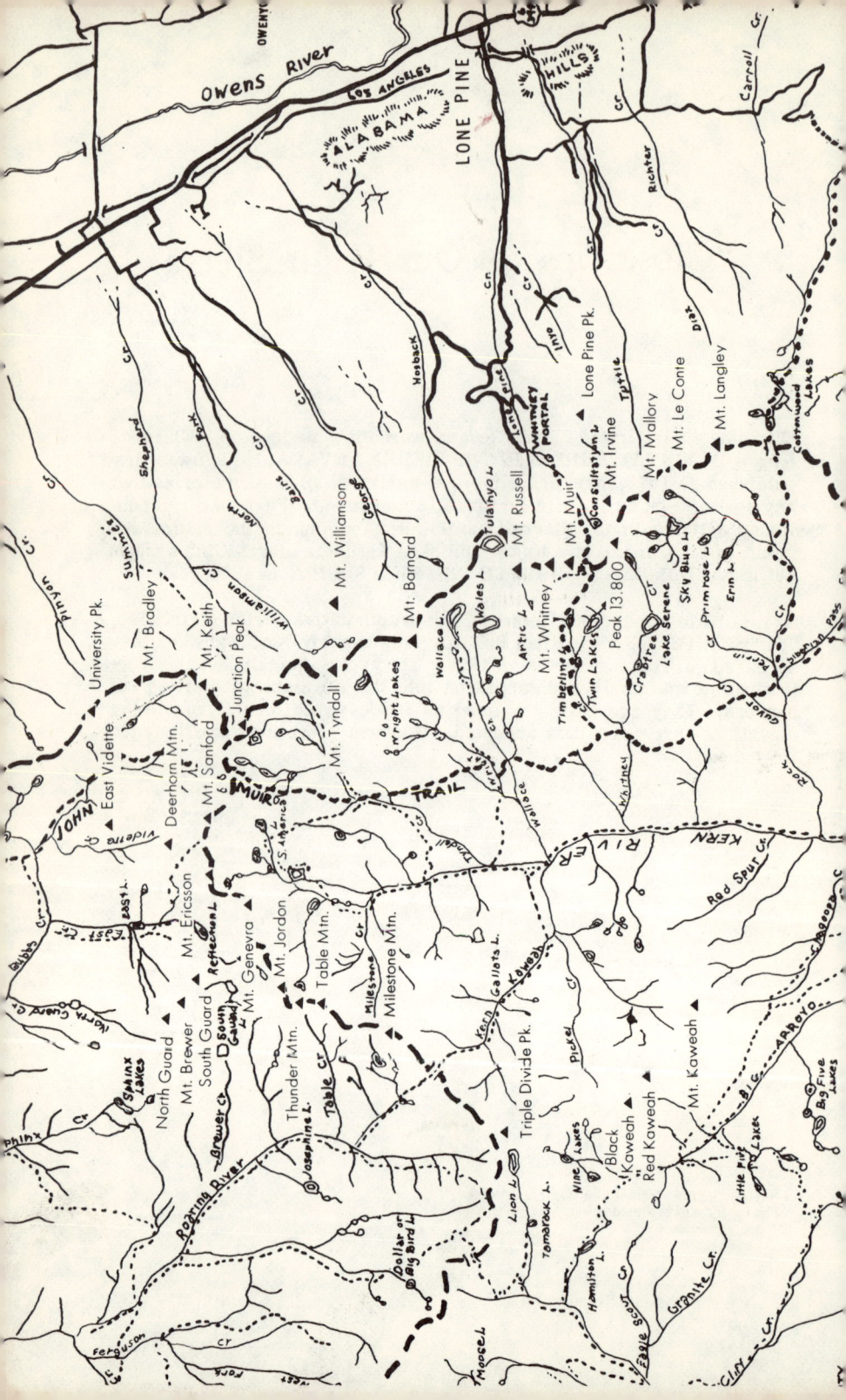

North Palisade

14,000-foot Peaks

FEW CALIFORNIANS know even the names of the 14,000-foot peaks of the Sierra Nevada, their knowledge of them being usually limited to the fact that Mt. Whitney is the highest mountain in the continental United States. Few are aware that there are ten others, all of which have at least one feature of interest.

They are either scenically attractive, afford exceptionally fine views from their summits, offer mountaineering inducements or possess all of these characteristics. All are found along the axis of the range from a point west of Lone Pine to one in the same direction from Big Pine. All may be said to be included in three groups which we may call those of Mt. Whitney, Mt. Williamson and the Palisades, from the most prominent mountain in each of them.

In this sketch we shall begin with the first of these. Many appear to be disappointed with the views ordinarily obtained of Mt. Whitney. Viewed from the Owens Valley to the east, other considerably lower peaks, due to their position seem to rival or even exceed it in height, while from the Kern region to the west, the comparatively gentle slope of that face of the mountain appears to rob it of spectacular features. However, both of these estimates appear to be in some degree unwarranted, for as one approaches Mt. Whitney from the east, its series of granite pinnacles stand in beautiful perspective at the head of Lone Pine

Canyon, a fine gorge walled in on either side throughout most of its length by high granite cliffs, while if one surveys it from the summit of any of the peaks of the Great Western Divide, the depth and the breath of the valley of the Kern seem to impart to it a grandeur that it appears to lack when beheld from nearer points in that direction.

B UT IT is from seldom-trodden vantage points that Mt.Whitney is most imposing. From Lone Pine Peak, Mts. Mallory and Irvine, Le Conte and Langley to the east and south; from Mts. Russell, Barnard and others to the north, Mt. Whitney is spectacular to a degree that would surprise those who have seen it only from the usual viewpoints.

The panorama beheld from Mt. Whitney is one of great extent and magnificence. To the north it extends along the axis of the range to the mountains of Yosemite; to the west it looks across the Kern basin to the castellated Kaweahs and the jagged line of the Kern-Kaweah divide; to the south, over gradually lowering forest-clad mountains; to the east and southeast, over a multitude of arid ranges and desert valleys.

Mt. Whitney is regarded by mountaineers as being remarkably easy of ascent. From the west, aside from a chimney of about a thousand feet, it is a walk up comparatively gentle slopes. From the east it demands more endurance, requiring a person to be in good condition to climb it from timberline and return without suffering from overexertion.

The last of the high pinnacles on the ridge running south from Mt. Whitney is called Mt. Muir. It attains an elevation of 14,025 feet. As one comes up the Mt. Whitney trail from the east, its sheer face and sharp summit are very striking. The summit commands an excellent view, especially of the rugged mountains to the southeast. It rises several hundred feet above the trail that winds along to the west of it, and necessitates a short but interesting rockclimb to reach it.

A FEW miles to the southeast of Mt. Whitney is Mt. Langley, 14,042 feet in elevation and the southernmost of the 14,000-foot peaks of the Sierra. In form it is similar to Mt. Whitney, as it slopes up gradually from the south and the southwest and breaks off in sheer precipices to the north and east. The view from its summit is very good but does not equal that from those farther to the north. The ascent from the south is extremely easy — in fact, a horse can be ridden to the summit from that direction. From the northwest it offers somewhat of a rock climb.

Immediately to the north of Mt. Whitney across a deep cirque, is Mt. Russell, 14,190 feet in altitude. It is a fine, craggy mountain, one that delights the heart of a mountaineer, and has been ascended fewer times than any other 14,000-foot peak in the Sierra Nevada. The ascent can be made from several directions, but is foolhardy for any but experienced mountaineers to climb it.

Its summit possesses one of the finest views obtainable of Mt. Whitney, as it looks directly across a chasm-like depression to the precipitous northern face of the latter. The view northward along the crest of the range westward over the Kern is magnificent.

M T. WILLIAMSON, about twelve miles north of Mt. Whitney, is one of the finest of the 14,000-foot peaks. Being only slightly lower than Mt. Whitney — 14,384 feet — and rising directly from the valley floor, it is probably the most spectacular mountain of all the range as viewed from Owens Valley. Its handsome deeply-fluted, cathedral-like mass is especially picturesque from the east and the north, while from the crest of the Sierra it is one of the most conspicuous and can be seen from almost every prominent elevation. The panorama visible from its summit is one of the finest in the Sierra, equaling, if not surpassing, that from Mt. Whitney, while its ascent is considerably more difficult than that of its loftier neighbor to the south.

A mile or so west of Mt. Williamson is Mt. Tyndall, (14,025). Its steep eastern face can be seen from Owens Valley, just to the north of the former. A fine view is to be had from its summit, especially of the great amphitheatre of lofty mountains that encircle the upper Kern Basin. The ascent is an easy matter, despite Clarence King's hair-raising story. From the northwest the climber works his way up some 2000 feet of talus rock and then along about 200 yards of narrow arête to the summit.

FOR SOME forty miles northward along the crest from Mt. Williamson there occur no 14,000-foot mountains. At this distance from it is the Palisade group, one of the finest in the Sierra. From the higher peaks all along the axis of the range from Mt. Whitney in the south to Mt. Lyell in the north, this cluster of serrated pinnacles and jagged ridges is conspicuous. Their southern faces rise abruptly — in most places sheer; their northern ones, with the exception of Split Mountain, are even more vertical. The North and Middle Palisades have been scaled from the south only; the South Palisade (Split Mountain) from the north only; Mt. Sill usually from the north.

The most beautiful mountain of these and one of the most beautiful in the Sierra is the North Palisade, whether one scans its jagged pinnacles from the south across granite gorges or across the Palisade Glacier and the basin to the north; it is one of the most striking peaks in the Sierra Nevada. Probably the view from its summit equals in scope and magnificence that obtained from any peak in the range and without being unusually hazardous or difficult, it is sufficiently so to render it interesting to the most skilled mountaineer.

About a mile to the east of the North Palisade is Mt. Sill, approximately 14,200 feet in elevation. It is an impressive mountain from the north and northeast, its sheer cliffs hundreds of feet in height facing these directions. It can be seen from Owens Valley in the vicinity of Big Pine. The view from its summit is fine but not quite equal to that of the North Palisade. Although a comparatively easy climb from the south, few have ever made the ascent. It can also be scaled from the Palisade Glacier by

Split Mountain
Photo by Tom Ross

14

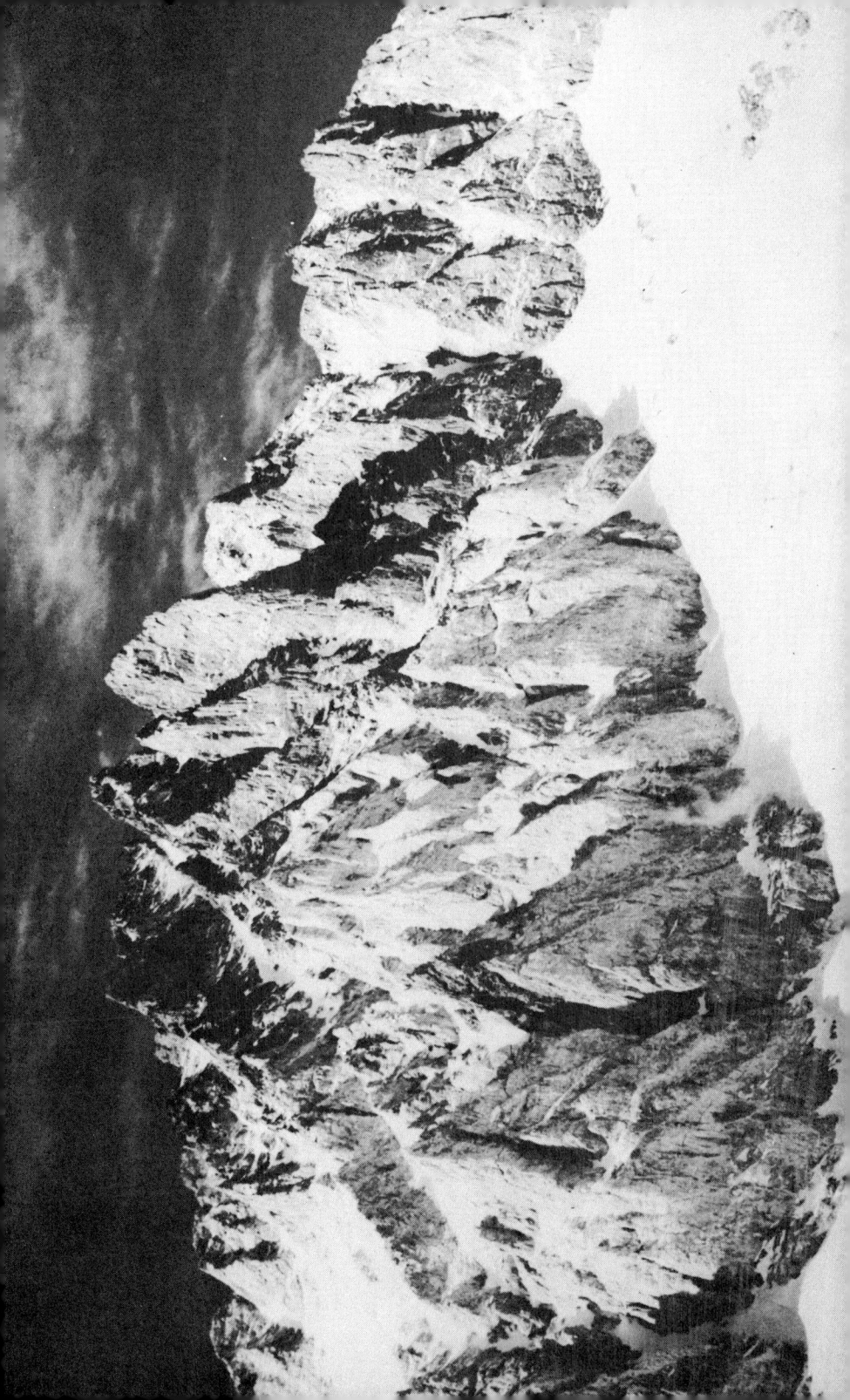

those experienced in rock-climbing.

Somewhat farther to the southeast is the Middle Palisade, 14,049 feet in elevation, the second of the group in scenic beauty and possibly the first in mountaineering difficulty. From the south it presents an imposing array of crags and pinnacles; from the north it is even more impressive as it rises in sheer cliffs above a steep glacier at the head of a deep canyon. There is an especially fine view of it looking up the south fork of Big Pine Creek about a half-mile west of Glacier Lodge. The panorama seen from its summit is inferior to that of those of this group already mentioned, but contains more of the great eastern escarpment of the Sierra. It has been scaled few times and only from the south; it is essentially a crag-and-chimney climb and is not recommended for novices. The summit itself is a ragged knife-edge about a hundred yards in length.

A few miles farther to the southeast, so far as sometimes to be regarded as not belonging to this group, is the South Palisade or Split Mountain, 14,051 feet in elevation. It is visible from the high peaks to the south and is the most colorful of the 14,000-foot peaks, the great cliffs of its southern and eastern faces displaying broad bands and extensive areas of red, orange, brown and other tints, while the summit forms a great capping of dark gray granite. It is very striking from Owens Valley, a few miles north of Independence.

THE PANORAMA seen from its summit ranks among the fine ones of the range. It is scalable from the north only, as the other faces of the mountain are sheer cliffs. From this direction it is very readily ascended, but due to its inaccessibility few have ever stood on the summit.

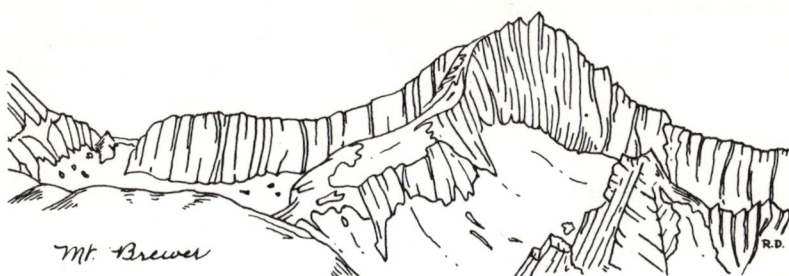

Mt. Brewer

13,500-14,000-foot Peaks

BOTH FROM a scenic and from a mountaineering standpoint many of the finest peaks of the Sierra Nevada range from 13,000 feet above sea-level to a trifle less than 14,000 feet. It seems to the writer that from neither of these viewpoints is the Sierra Nevada adequately appreciated, for the Sierra is not only one of the most imposing ranges in the United States en masse but also contains many individual peaks of great beauty and numbers whose ascent requires considerable mountaineering skill and daring. In both of these respects there are probably more noteworthy peaks within the range of elevation spoken of above than any other of similar radius in the Sierra. Beginning with the most southerly in the range, I shall briefly review some of the most outstanding of them.

As one looks westward from the vicinity of Lone Pine he observes a jagged line of pinnacles along the crest of the Sierra, that gradually increases in height from the south to the north, to the highest which attains an elevation of 13,960 feet. This is Mt. Le Conte. If it is impressive when beheld from Owens Valley, it is much more so when seen from nearby peaks across deep cirques which greatly enhance the striking appearance of this array of giant pinnacles that rise sheer for hundreds of feet. In the matter of ascent it ranks among the more difficult peaks of the Sierra and has been climbed but twice. Nearby to the north and northwest are Mts. Mallory, Irvine and Peak 13,800 that have been scaled but few times — the last but once. The first two are especially noteworthy on account of the excellent views that they afford of the precipitous eastern front of Mt. Whitney.

FROM almost any of the higher elevations of the southern Sierra, one can descry the splendid group of the Kaweahs, situated westward from Mt. Whitney across the Kern basin. They attain an average elevation of about 13,700 feet and form one of the most beautiful and spectacular groups in all the Sierra. They include Mt. Kaweah, the Red, Gray and Black Kaweahs. To the north, the sheer walls of all of them rise above a great cirque; to the south and west, three of them have an easy approach up one face, with the exception of the Black Kaweah which is sheer on all sides. In their beautifully serrated lines they are among the most conspicuous mountains in the Sierra; in richness of coloring, they are the finest in the Kern Region and among the finest in the range. In all, except the Black Kaweah — which in most lights is a gleaming black — the prevailing color is a rich red.

Like the Palisades farther to the north, they have the distinction of being picturesque, no matter from what direction they may be viewed; or whether from far or near. Close at hand, they are especially striking from the Five Lakes Basin and the Chagoopa Plateau to the south, and from the elevations about the upper Kern-Kaweah to the north. From almost all points in the upper Kern region this cluster of peaks stands out superbly picturesque, while seen from the high peaks far up the range, they form one of the most beautiful landmarks in the Sierra. All of the main peaks but the Black Kaweah are easy of ascent. The last is regarded as one of the most difficult and dangerous peaks of the high Sierra, and its summit can be reached only by climbing a long chimmney running up its southern face.

Slightly to the west of the Kaweahs, extending north and south past them, is the Kern-Kaweah or Great Western Divide. It was once the main crest of the Sierra and is now remarkable

18

for the extreme ruggedness and variation of the forms of the peaks of which it is composed. It is a long line of spiry, pyramidal and mesa-like peaks that are extremely impressive as they stand silhouetted against a blue sky, or as billowy clouds hover about their ragged crest. The most noteworthy of these is Milestone Mountain. It is essentially a pyramid surmounted by a slender flat-topped spire several hundred feet in height and attaining an altitude of 13,643 feet above sea-level. Apparently inaccessible on all sides, it is actually so on three of them, but the western side — despite its formidable wall-like appearance — can be scaled with comparative ease. This vulnerable face can be approached from the south, the north — with difficulty — or from the east by crossing the crest on either side of the great obelisk that forms the summit. It is regarded as one of the finest viewpoints in the Sierra. To the south, the Kaweahs; to the east, across the Kern Basin, the great peaks of the main crest of the Sierra; to the north and northeast, those of the Kings-Kern divide form a panorama of the most rugged sublimity.

NORTHWARD a short distance from Milestone Mountain is Table Mountain, 13,646 feet in elevation. It is a great, flat-topped mountain whose sides in most places seem almost vertical. Although comparatively easy of ascent from the south along narrow shelves and up a rocky chimney, it has been climbed but few times. It can also be surmounted by forcing one's way up a precipitous chimney on its northern face and over several hundred feet of broken, steeply sloping wall above it, but this route is likely to entail a good deal of snow and perhaps some ice-climbing. The summit slants down gently to the south and it is both novel and interesting to walk across it, or around its border that drops away in most places in sheer precipices.

In striking contrast to the mesa-like form of Table Mountain is the slender pyramid of Thunder Mountain (13,578 feet) only a short distance to the north of it — one of the finest examples in the Sierra of what one might call the Gothic type. Its summit tapers to three slender spires, one of which is somewhat higher

than the others and only a few feet in diameter at its highest point. It commands an excellent view and has probably been scaled but twice.

Northward a few miles from Thunder Mountain is Mt. Brewer, 13,555 feet in height. It can be readily climbed from the northeast, the south and the west, and possesses one of the best views obtainable in the Sierra. From the north especially it is a remarkably beautiful peak, its broadly pyramidal lines and vertical northern face being visible far up the range, and together with the North and South Guards on either side of it, forms one of the most imposing groups in the Sierra.

ALONG the Kings-Kern divide, slightly to the south of Mt. Brewer, are numbers of lofty peaks, the finest of which is Mt. Stanford, 13,983 feet in altitude. Its wide, massive form is seen to best advantage from the north across the great amphitheatre in that direction, but its southwestern cliffs are very impressive from the western portion of the upper Kern Basin. It has twin peaks of almost equal height, the northern one being perhaps a few feet the higher. The most southerly of these can be readily scaled from the Upper Kern, but few care to traverse the ragged knife-edge that connects it with the more northerly one. Other worth-while peaks along the Kings-Kern divide are Junction Peak (13,903 feet) and Mt. Ericcson (13,625 feet). Neither has been climbed frequently and the former affords good rock-climbing up a knife-edge from the east; the latter, up its eastern face.

Along the main crest, to the east of the upper Kings amphitheatre, are two peaks over 13,500 feet in altitude; Mt. Keith (13,990 feet) and University Peak (13,588 feet). The former can easily be climbed from Junction Pass; the later can be scaled from Bullfrog Lake, Vidette Meadow to the west, or from the Matlock Lakes and the head of a canyon to the east. The view obtained from the summit is extremely fine. University Peak is a very beautiful and imposing mountain when seen from Kearsarge Peak to the northeast and from Independence Peak to the

Peaks of the Kings Canyon Region.

east. From University Peak to Split Mountain, a distance of some fifteen miles in an air-line, there occur no peaks with an altitude of 13,500 feet or over. Just to the north of the last named are several seldom-climbed ones, including Bolton Brown Mountain, Birch Mountain, The Thumb and others.

IN THE northern portion of the Palisade group are two unusually fine ones in Mt. Winchell and Agassiz Needle.* Both are scalable from the Palisade Glacier; the former being an excellent but not dangerous rock climb; the latter, a comparatively easy one. Agassiz Needle can be scaled up its eastern face — a somewhat hazardous feat — and up its western slope, a very easy one. Both afford superb views, especially of the Palisades and northeast across the Palisade amphitheatre.

Some fifteen miles to the northwest of the Palisades is the Evolution group, an unusually interesting one containing a dozen or more peaks surrounding a basin about six miles in length of the same name. The best of these are Mts. Goddard and Darwin. The broad, dark cone of the first, 13,841 feet in elevation, is a conspicuous landmark far to the north and south along the crest of the range. Due to its central and somewhat isolated position at the southeastern end of Evolution Basin, it possesses one of the most extensive views that can be had in the Sierra — one commanding the main axis of the range from Mt. Whitney to Mt. Lyell. The ascent is rather easy and can be made from the Evolution Basin to the north; the upper San Joaquin to the west and from the headwaters of Goddard Creek to the south.

ALONG the crest to the northeast of the basin is the great, flat-topped Mt. Darwin. Its walls are vertical almost everywhere and can be scaled from only two directions — across a glacier on its northern flank and along a knife-edge to the summit; up a tangle of chimneys on its southwestern face and thence by the same arête to the top. The highest point of the mountain is a slender turret just to the east of the main peak. Few have ascended the latter and still fewer the former. Mt. Darwin is considered to be one of the difficult mountains of the

*Renamed Mt. Agassiz.

Sierra, and one possessing a very fine view.

As one looks northwestward from the summit of Mt. Darwin, he descies, within a distance of ten miles, a rather solitary peak rising from the verge of a wide, timberless basin mostly above an elevation of 11,000 feet. It is Mt. Humphreys. The mountain possesses an unusually stern and almost forbidding aspect. It is generally rated as one of the most difficult of the higher peaks of the Sierra Nevada, and although comparatively accessible, only about twenty-five humans have stood on its summit.

NORTHWARD a few miles from Mt. Humphreys is Mt. Tom a beautiful, symmetrical mountain when viewed from the summit of Mt. Humphreys, the South Fork of Bishop Creek, Owens Valley or from the summit of Bear Creek Spire and other peaks to the northwest. Its richness of coloring, chiefly soft reds and browns, is very pleasing to the eye. The ascent presents no mountaineering difficulties, but is rather long, as the usual starting points are at comparatively low elevations.

To the northwest of Mt. Tom, across a profound gorge looms a sharp, pyramidal mountain, 13,708 feet in elevation. This is Bear Creek Spire, perhaps the finest of a number of peaks that encircle a treeless, granite basin containing Lake Italy. This basin is locked away in the Sierra in such a fashion that few have ever seen it. Lake Italy is a beautiful lake with rugged granite peaks springing up in every direction. Except for a few stunted albicaulis pines clinging to slopes with unusually favorable exposures, the valley is entirely devoid of trees.

Bear Creek Spire rises at the northeastern corner of the basin. Perhaps the most striking views of it are from the north, up Little Lakes Basin. It is an unusually impressive mountain of the Matterhorn type. On all sides, except the west, it drops away in almost vertical walls hundreds of feet in height. The summit itself is a single monolith only a few feet in diameter from which these jagged arêtes radiate in true Matterhorn fashion. It has been scaled twice up its western face. On that side it slopes up gradually until within about a hundred and fifty feet of the summit, where a rock wall of considerable difficulty must be negotiated. The last rock, projecting above a narrow knife-edge with a drop of 500 feet in one direction and 150 feet in the other, being of rather smooth granite and reaching a height that one can scarcely reach over and with no holds on its flanks except one or two shallow cip-like depressions, requires steady nerves.

The view obtained from this circumscribed perch is superb. To the east, across deep gorges, is Mt. Tom; to the south, beyond others, is the lofty and commanding form of Mt. Humphreys; to the south, Seven Gables, Mt. Hilgard and other rugged peaks; to the west, across Lake Italy Basin, Mt. Gabb; to the northwest, the group containing Mts. Dade, Abbot and Mills.

ANOTHER handsome mountain as one looks up the Rock Creek Basin is Mt. Dade. To the north it breaks away in sheer cliffs at whose base lies a small glacier. It can be readily climbed from Italy Basin, which is reached from upper Rock Creek by crossing a saddle to the east of the peak. It has been ascended only a few times, although the view from its summit is a very good one. It looks directly across Italy Basin to Seven Gables and far north and south along the crest of the range.

West of Mt. Dade, and joined to it by a sharp knife-edge is Mt. Abbot (13,736). It can be ascended by scrambling up a chimney on its southern face and may possibly be climbed from the head-waters of Rock Creek. To the west of Italy Basin and occupying a somewhat isolated position is Mt. Gabb (13,701). It is an easy climb and its summit commands a fine prospect. The fact that none of the Abbot group is climbed frequently is due largely to their standing to the side of the main lines of travel in the Sierra Nevada. They rise in a somewhat remote and sequestered region which possesses a certain charm all its own. In every direction they overlook high granite basins for thr most part above timberline. As one looks up upper Rock Creek Basin, Bear Creek Spire and Mts. Dade and Abbot form a superb sky-

Bear Creek Spire
Photo by Norman Clyde

24

line of jagged peaks.

To the southeast of upper Rock Creek Basin is Mt. Morgan (13,739). It also has been climbed but a few times, notwithstanding the fact that its summit affords a sublime view across great gorges, far down the crest of the Sierras; northward past the richly colored mountains about Convict Lake to the Yosemite Mountains beyond them.

With the above peaks the 13,500 foot peaks of the Sierra terminate, the loftiest of those to the north being slightly over 13,000 feet in elevation. Although less than 14,000 feet in elevation, they are mountains of which California may well be proud, for their picturesqueness, for the magnificent views obtained from their summits and for the opportunities for strenuous but beautiful mountaineering which they afford.

Temple Crag

13,000-13,500-foot Peaks

ALTHOUGH THE majority of the finer peaks of the southern Sierra rise to elevations exceeding 13,500 feet, yet many of them do not attain that altitude, a considerable number being between 13,000 and 13,500 feet above sea-level. It might be observed, however, that height is only one element in the appraisal of a mountain, whether from a scenic or from a mountaineering standpoint. Mt. Whitney, for example, as fine a mountain as it may be, is excelled in picturesqueness by many lower mountains in the Sierra, and the ascent, except for the rarity of air near the summit, is generally conceded to be very easy.

Along the more southerly portion of the Great Western Divide, on the Kings-Kern Divide and along the main crest overlooking Owens Valley, there are a few peaks within the elevation specified in this sketch. To the southwest of Lone Pine Peak — is an unnamed peak, 13,016 feet in altitude. Although not a conspicuous one, it affords the best view to be had of Mt. Le Conte, whose line of jagged pinnacles towers to the south across a deep narrow gorge; an excellent one of Mt. Langley, with sheer northern and eastern precipices beyond it; of Mts. Mallory and Irvine to the west, and of Mt. Whitney to the northwest. The summit is a ragged knife-edge that presents some difficulties to the climber and has been scaled probably but once.

On the Kings-Kern Divide there are two which might be included,

TOURING TOPICS, June 1928

Mt. Genevra (13,037) and Mt. Jordon (13,136). Both are easy of ascent, afford fine prospects and being near the junction of the Kings-Kern and the Kern-Kaweah divides, possess an excellent view of both as well as of the great amphitheatre to the north.

CUTTING northward from about the middle of the Kings-Kern divide is Deerhorn Mountain, a beautiful peak consisting of a line of granite spires, the highest of which is 13,440 feet in elevation. It is one of the finest "crag" mountains of the Sierra. The best view of it is obtained from the vicinity of Bullfrog Lake looking southward past the East Vidette and across the amphitheatre, from which it stands out as one of the most striking peaks along the divide, although others exceed it considerably in height. Its craggy structure is seen to best advantage to the south of Harrison Pass and the top of Mt. Ericcson. Its summit affords the best view obtainable of the crags of Mt. Ericcson, immediately to the south across a bowl-shaped cirque. Although probably scaled but once, the ascent is not especially difficult for one experienced in rock-climbing.

Mt. Brewer, one of the most attractive of Sierra peaks, has a peak on either flank, called respectively the North and South Guards. The former, 13,304 feet in altitude, is a fine rock-climb, and has had only one ascent, and that dubious, as the climber did not scale a granite monolith some twenty feet in height which may be the highest point and which, without hand- or foot-holds, leans in an embarrassing way over a five-hundred foot precipice. There is also some difference of opinion as to whether the South Guard is Spire 12,964 or Peak 13,232 to the south of the former. Both are easily climbed and both afford good views. The first has probably been climbed but once.

Between Mt. Keith and University Peak on the main crest to the east of the upper Kings amphitheatre is Mt. Bradley, 13,320 feet in elevation. It is a somewhat impressive peak as seen from Owens Valley, near Independence, and can be climbed from that side if one has sufficient patience to work his way up the rugged, trail-less canyon of Piñon Creek. Most of the few ascents that

Mt. Goddard
Photo by Norman Clyde

28

have been made, however, were from the upper portion of Center Basin to the west of the peak. It commands an excellent view.

Just to the north of Kearsarge Pass is Mt. Gould (13,001), worthy of noting on account of its accessibility and the fine panorama seen from its summit. The ascent is an easy 1200-foot scamble from the pass and the view extends from Mt. Williamson in the south to the Evolution and Abbot groups in the north. The sight of scores of peaks from the summit in winter, arrayed in splendid snowy garb, is grand almost beyond description.

R AE LAKE possesses one of the most wildly picturesque settings of any in the Sierra, consisting of numerous rugged peaks, several of which exceed 13,000 feet in elevation. Of these Black and Diamond Peaks might be mentioned. Neither is difficult of ascent; neither has been climbed more than a few times and both overlook deep, narrow gorges and ragged ridges, composed largely of dark schists and slates, in which a few mountain sheep still linger, although they are seldom seen except when winter snows drive them far down the eastern slope of the Sierra toward Owens Valley. A few miles farther north is Baxter Peak. The view from the more easterly of its two peaks down the great eastern scarp of the Sierra, is very impressive.

A very interesting but seldom-visited portion of the Sierra is the upper basin of the south fork of the Kings River. It is largely above timberline, is some miles in extent and is surrounded by mountains, some of which are above 13,000 feet and one — Split Mountain — over 14,000 feet. Excepting the latter, the most outstanding peak around the basin is Pinchot, 13,471 feet in elevation. It is also the most conspicuous of a number of deeply-colored mountains of this part of the range, owing their reds and browns to slates and schists surviving from the sedimentary deposits that once covered the Sierra. Their warmth of hue is an agreeable change from the uniform gray tones that usually obtain in the granite, which is the preponderating rock in the range.

N

BISHOP

BIG PI

US 395

Owens River

Klondike L.

Waren L.

Freeman Cr.

Rawson Cr.

East Fork Coyote Cr.

Baker Cr.

Big Pine Cr.

Birch Cr.

Little
Brainard L.

North Palisade
Mt. Sill
Mt. Winchill
Temple Crag
Agassiz Needle

Birch Cr.

Bishop Cr.

McGee Cr.

Horton L.

Mt. Horton

Mt. Tom

Mt. Humphreys

Green L.
Baker L.
Brown L.
South L.
Long L.
Mt. Thompson
Mt. Gilbert
Mt. Powell

L. Sabrina
George L.
Blue L.

Mt. Emerson
North L.
Piute L.
Lamarck Cr.

Helen L.
MUIR PASS

PIUTE PASS
Muriel L.

Mt. Darwin
Mt. Spencer
Sapphire L.
Mt. Haeckel
Mt. Wallace
Mt. Huxley
Mt. McGee
Wanda L.

The Hermit
Evolution
Davis L.

Mt. Goddard

JOHN MUIR TRAIL

Martha L.

Mt. Dade
Mt. Gabb
L. Italy
Bear Creek Spire
Pine L.
Morgan Cr.
ITALY PASS
Hilgard Mt.
Hilgard
Bear Cr.

Seven Gables

Royce Lakes
Desolation L.
Pilot Knob

Piute Cr.

SCALE IN MILES

JUST TO the north of Mt. Pinchot is Striped Mountain (13,160), so named from the contorted bands of schist and quartzite which compose a large portion of its metamorphic mass. Interesting rock-work can be had up its steeper faces, but it is not what would be called a difficult mountain.

North of Striped Mountain, across Taboose Pass, is Cardinal Mountain (13,388), deriving its name from a capping of cardinal schist and slate that forms a considerable portion of it and extends northward in a conspicuous layer along the crest of the arête that connects it with Split Mountain. The ascent is extremely easy and the view obtained is an excellent one, especially of the deep cirque to the north, across which frowns the great furrowed face of Split Mountain, banded with red, orange and black.

Although the main peaks of the Palisade group reach elevations greater than 13,500 feet, there are several lower ones that are extremely picturesque and which afford excellent climbing. The finest of these summits is Temple Crag (Mt. Alice), 13,016 feet in height. It is doubtful whether there is a more beautiful and striking "crag-mountain" in the Sierra Nevada. Its northern and northeastern faces are sheer precipices varied by numbers of spiry, turret-like, pinnacles beautifully placed.

The ascent is a thrilling, but not especially dangerous, rock-climb, and has been accomplished several times. The view at its summit is circumscribed, but as the crag stands near the center of the Palisade amphitheatre it affords, perhaps, the best view to be had of this great cirque walled in to the south by the magnificent Palisades, whose dark serrated forms rise from a series of glaciers that cling to their bases and send icy fingers far up the steep chutes that furrow their northern fronts. To the west of Temple Crag and connected with it by an impassable knife-edge is an unnamed pinnacle 13,400 feet in altitude, which commands a very fine view of the Palisades and offers an interesting rock-climb up its northwestern face. It has probably been climbed but once.

IN THE Evolution Basin — a mountain-encircled oval depression some six or eight miles in length containing the headwaters of a tributary of the south fork of the San Joaquin — there are several peaks between 13,000 and 13,500 feet worthy of note. Looking southward across Evolution Lake, one is impressed by Mts. Spencer and Huxley, sharp, granite peaks, the latter 13,124 feet in height. Both stand well out toward the middle of the basin so that their summits command a very good panorama of the wild, craggy mountains that encircle them. Mt. Huxley is an excellent rockclimb that is not attended by any especial danger or difficulty.

Along the line of peaks bordering the basin to the east, is Mt. Haeckel (13,422), a very beautiful peak tapering to a narrow point — a fine example of what might be termed a Gothic type of peak, not uncommon in the Sierra Nevada. Nearby are other similar ones, including Mt. Wallace and several unnamed ones to the east. They are impressive, seen from Evolution Basin, but still more so, looking from the northeast up the amphitheatre of the middle fork of Bishop Creek, as they form a beautiful and inspiring group of sharp peaks — snow-splashed in summer, snow-clad in winter — with Mt. Haeckel the outstanding member of the cluster, It is a fairly difficult climb that has been negotiated several times. To the northeast of the amphitheatre are several flat-topped peaks somewhat above 13,000 feet in elevation. Among these are Mts. Gilbert, Thompson and Powell. They form a striking portion of an almost complete circle of mountains about the middle fork of Bishop Creek and have seldom been scaled.

When one nears Piute Pass from the east, he is flanked on either side by two fine peaks — Mt. Emerson to the right and an unnamed one to the left. The first can be climbed by following any one of a number of steep chutes that run up its southern face, and on its summit a good view is obtained, especially of Mt. Humphreys, which looms grandly across a cirque to the northwest. It is an imposing peak from an elevation to the south and southeast and displays more or less of a warm red hue that increases in depth in a long line of pinnacles that run eastward from it. Seen from the Puite trail, the other peak is both beautiful and striking. Probably neither peak has been climbed more than once.

S ITUATED in a rather isolated position on the headwaters of Bear Creek and attaining an altitude of 13,066 feet is Seven Gables. It is a conspicuous mountain, from any direction, and on account of its position a wide view is obtained from its summit. Several miles northward from Seven Gables is Mt. Hilgard (13,351), one of a circle of peaks that surround Italy Basin. It is easy of ascent and commands a good prospect far and near, overlooking the barren but attractive depression of Lake Italy Basin to the northeast; the interesting region of Bear Creek and the Vermilion Cliffs nearby to the northwest, while its more extensive panorama extends far up and down the range. Northward from Mt. Hilgard a few miles is Mt. Mills (13,353), a peak that rises in very rugged surroundings, is an attractive climb, and has probably not been scaled more than once.

As one looks northward from the summit of any of the last-named peaks, he descries, not many miles distant, a group of softly-colored mountains whose reds and browns delight the eye, surmounted by one considerably higher, Red Slate Mountain, a readily climbed peak that overlooks a wide panorama. North of this group the Sierra drops down in a deep depression, to rise again in the Ritter and Lyell groups, belonging to the mountains of the Yosemite region, beyond the limits of the Southern Sierra.

T HE SCENIC character of a mountain, after all, and its spectacular aspects, depend more on the close juxtaposition of height and depression rather than upon mere elevation. There is little apparent difference between a precipice with a thousand-foot sheer declivity and one that falls away for fifteen hundred feet. Hence many of the most imposing of Sierra peaks will be found in the 13,000-13,500-foot group.

34

Snow Peak.

R.D.

12,000 - foot Peaks.

C OMPARED WITH the great number of peaks in the Southern
Sierra ranging from 13,000 to 14,501 feet in elevation — upwards of a hundred and fifty — those that do not attain an altitude
of 13,000 feet appear to be relatively low and sometimes almost
insignificant, yet scattered along this portion of the range there
are many fine peaks between 12,000 and 13,000 feet in height —
peaks striking in appearance, difficult to scale and affording excellent views from their summits. On account of the great average elevation of the Kern region they are perhaps fewest in this
portion of the Sierra, yet even there are found some worthy of
mention.

In the more southerly portion of the Great Western Divide are
many peaks that afford interesting climbs and good views, especially of the Kaweahs, a beautiful cluster of peaks that dom-
inates the Kern region to the west of the Kern River. Perhaps
the best of these is Sawtooth Peak (12,340). Its sharp pyramidal summit can be seen far down the western slope of the
range and in clear winter weather can be identified from the San
Joaquin Valley and perhaps even from the summit of the Coast
Range. It forms a worthy introduction to the High Sierra for
those entering the Sierra by way of Cliff Creek and over Black
Rock Pass. Farther north on the same divide, northwest of the
Kaweahs, is Triple Divide Peak (12,651), one that affords some
rock-climbing, is a rather impressive pyramid-like peak and

commands a fine panorama.

From its summit the view of the precipitous north face of the Kaweahs is superb, as is also the one along the jagged line of Kern-Kaweah divide; of the sheer cliffs on the western front of some of them and of the cirques, often adorned with Alpine tarns that appear far below. Very pleasing also is the sight of the dark undulating conifer forest, in which one can descry in the distance the Giant Forest, and far beyond it the hazy San Joaquin Valley.

ON THE opposite side of the range overlooking Owens Valley is Lone Pine Peak, slightly under 13,000 feet in height. From the valley, on account of standing well out in the great eastern scarp, it is one of the most striking peaks in the vicinity, vying with considerably higher neighbors. It has probably not been ascended more than two or three times, although it can be scaled with comparative ease from the headwaters of the south fork of Lone Pine Creek. The view from the summit is very fine, especially of Mt. Whitney and the eastern scarp of the Sierra, of which this peak possesses an unobstructed view northward for some fifty miles of the highest portion of the range.

In the Kings watershed noteworthy 12,000-foot peaks are more numerous. Perhaps the most beautiful of them is the East Vidette (12,742). Seen from the north, especially from Vidette Meadow and the vicinity of Bullfrog Lake, there is perhaps no peak in the Sierra possessing more pleasing lines that converge from a broad base to a narrow summit, forming a symmetrical pyramid with a beautifully furrowed front. Its sober gray color is set off by a mantle of dark foxtail and tamarack pine that sweeps up from the meadow at its base to its precipitous walls. The ascent is a rock-climb of some difficulty that has been made about a dozen times. On account of its central position, the summit commands a magnificent view of the great jagged peaks that extend around the amphitheatre in an almost complete circle.

Mts. Spencer and Huxley
Photo by Norman Clyde

36

On the divide between the Kings-Kern amphitheatre and the Rae Lake basin are several peaks deserving of mention, notably Mt. Rixford (12,856) and Mt. Gardiner (12,903). The ascent of the former entails some rock-work of a not very difficult nature, and the summit has an impressive view of the great amphitheatre to the south and of Rae Lake basin to the north, with its chain of beautiful lakes. Farther west along the same ridge, jutting out northward from it is Mt. Gardiner. Possessing sheer cliffs to the west and north, it is an impressive peak from these directions. It can be ascended only from the south, and then by crossing a saddle from a slightly lower peak, working up a broken rock face for about a hundred feet and thence along a ragged knife-edge to the highest point about fifty yards distant. It is regarded as a difficult peak and has been scaled but few times.

ONE OF the most sequested basins of the High Sierra is Rae Lake Basin. It contains a chain of lakes of which Rae Lake, the largest, is also the finest, being indeed one of the most beautiful and picturesque in all the range. Ensconced in a deep bowl, rugged mountains rising on all sides, those to the south and southwest richly colored red, orange and black, bands of which run in a most bizarre fashion; varied by rocky islets and promontories sparsely clad with tamarack pines, it has become one of the favorites of those who frequent the Sierra.

One of the most fantastically banded of these mountains is Dragon Peak (12,955), along the main crest of the range, to the northeast of the lake. It terminates in a sharp pinnacle which offers an interesting rock scramble that probably only two parties have made, and overlooks an extremely ragged and broken portion of the eastern escarpment of the Sierra.

A few miles to the northwest of the lake, from a basin dotted with Alpine tarns called Sixty Lake Basin, rises a rather solitary mountain of the Matterhorn type, a beautiful pyramid from whatever angle it may be viewed and generally conceded to be one of the most difficult ascents of the Sierra.

Peaks of the Mono Creek Region.

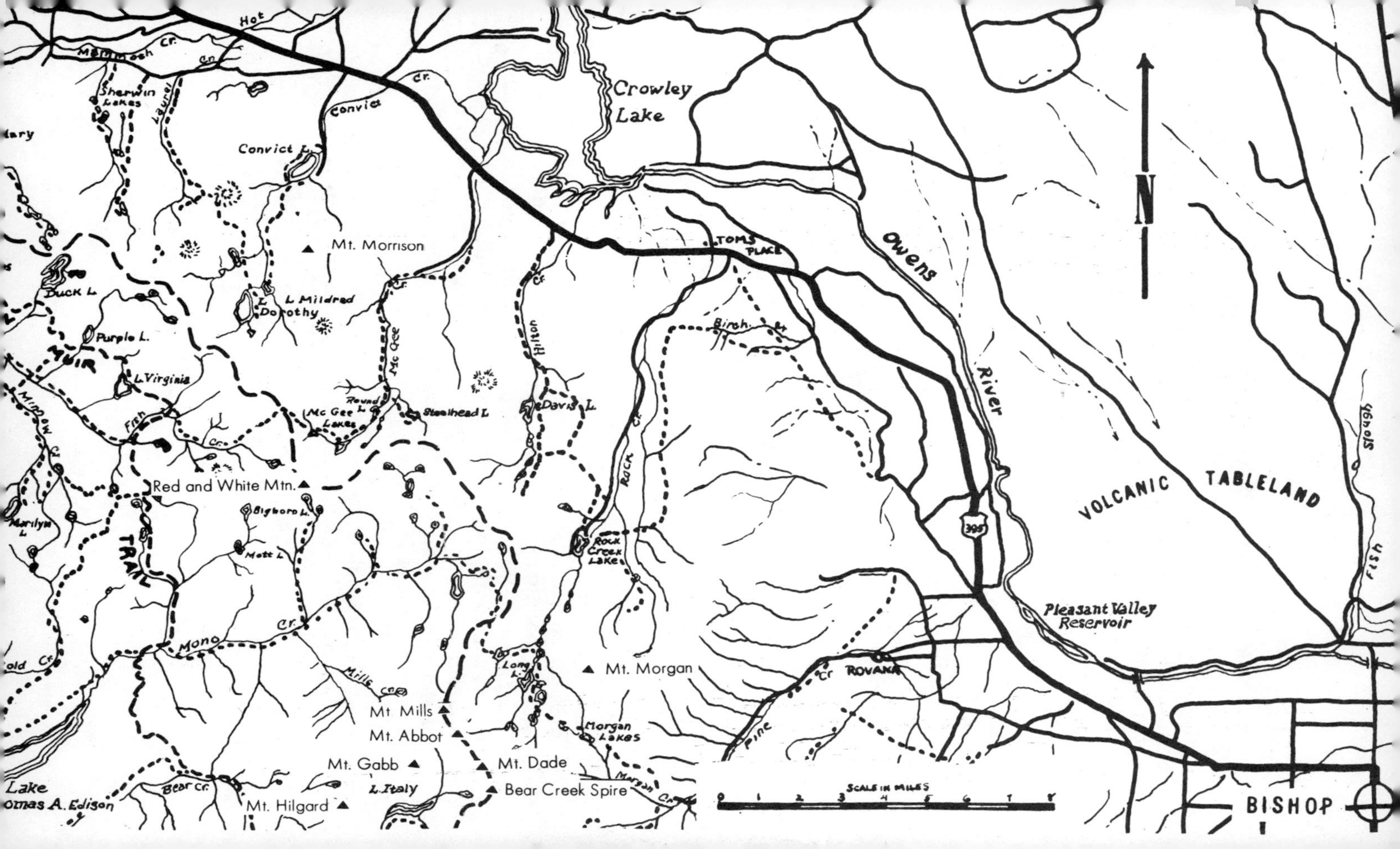
Hot
Mammoth Cr.
Cr.
Sherwin Lakes
Laurel
Convict
Cr.
Crowley Lake
Convict L.
Mt. Morrison
L. Mildred
Dorothy
Duck L.
Purple L.
Muir
L. Virginia
Minnow Cr.
Fish
Cr.
Round L.
Mc Gee Lakes
Mc Gee
Steelhead L.
Hilton
Cr.
Davis L.
TOMS PLACE
Owens
River
Birch Cr.
Rock Cr.
Rock Creek Lake
Red and White Mtn.
Bighorn L.
Mott L.
Marilyn L.
TRAIL
Mono
Cr.
Mills Cr.
Mt. Mills
Mt. Abbot
Mt. Gabb
Mt. Dade
Bear Creek Spire
Mt. Hilgard
L. Italy
Bear Cr.
Lake
Thomas A. Edison
Mt. Morgan
Long L.
Morgan Lakes
Morgan Cr.
395
VOLCANIC TABLELAND
Pleasant Valley Reservoir
Slough
Fish
N
Pine Cr.
ROVANA
SCALE IN MILES
0 1 2 3 4 5 6 7 8
BISHOP

This is Mt.King,* 12,909 feet in elevation. All the ascents except one, have been accomplished by following a narrow shelf that runs diagonally up the almost vertical eastern face of the mountain to a point a few rods below the summit. From there the climber hoists himself over large rocks to a little alcove above a steep precipice and perhaps fifteen feet below the summit. Here he is confronted by a vertical "pitch". After groping around he finds a fingerhold and a cup-like depression that forms a tolerably safe foothold. Swinging himself up he grasps the top of the rock above, conscious that the precipice awaits him if he should let go. Reaching the former safely he encounters a weather-polished rounded boulder over which he can reach a short distance.

U P THIS he scrambles and finds himself on the summit only a few feet in diameter. In three directions ragged knife-edges drop away; in two there are almost vertical precipices, while in the third it slopes down at a very steep angle. As it stands comparatively alone it possesses a much finer view than would be expected from its height. To the west it looks down into Paradise Valley, one of the most beautiful gorges in the Sierra; to the northeast by Mt. Pinchot, other nearby highly colored peaks are conspicuous, as are also the Palisades farther to the north and Mt. Goddard to the northwest; to the south the serrated line of the Kings-Kern Divide looms high across the intervening ridge. In the descent one can drop from shelf to shelf down the eastern face of the mountain for twenty or thirty feet until he strikes the other route. Mt. King is what mountaineers some - times term a "two-man" mountain — one which contains pitches that are difficult for a single mountaineer to surmount but may sometimes be negotiated without great trouble by a party of two or more by reason of mutual assistance. About ten have stood on the summit of Mt. King.

From Woods Lakes, a delightful group near Sawmill Pass, one can climb Colosseum Mountain (12,417), an easy ascent that possesses a good view. A short distance northward along the crest is Mt. Perkins (12,557), which has some rock-climbing and has probably been climbed but once. A charming camping

*Mt. Clarence King

place a few miles to the northwest is Bench Lake. As its name implies, it is situated on a bench overlooking the south fork of the Kings River only a few miles from its source. The rocky terrain to the north and the long promontories that jut out into the usually placid water of the lake and several rocky islets are clothed with a scattered growth of tamarack pines, while to the southwest rises a beautiful peak called Arrow Mountain, with symmetrical pyramidal form. From the lake it can be ascended with comparative ease and the climber is rewarded with a magnificent view.

PASSING northwestward to the Evolution group, one finds there also several interesting 12,000-foot peaks. North from Mt. Goddard is a dark, picturesque but somewhat forbidding peak — Mt. McGee, 12,966 feet in height; a rather difficult climb commanding an excellent view, especially down into Goddard Canyon, a beautiful tributary to the south fork of the San Joaquin River. Probably it has been climbed but twice. Northward several miles from it is The Hermit (12,352). Viewed from Colby Meadows to the northwest, it ranks among the most beautiful mountains in the Sierra. Its slender gray cone rises from a verdant meadow and the grove of tamarack pines and is especially striking when clouds hang about its narrow summit. The ascent is a rock climb of some difficulty, as the latter consists of a rounded monolith which is troublesome for a single mountaineer to surmount, as it is without holds and is higher than one can reach. It has been climbed several times.

Entering Evolution Basin from the north, ones attention is attracted by two striking peaks that rise picturesquely to the south beyond the curving expanse of Evolution Lake. They are Mts. Spencer and Huxley. The former is easily climbed and is a very good vantage-point from which to view the mountains around the Evolution Basin.

As one follows the trail up Piute Creek, a sharp pinnacle appears to block the way. It is very striking, especially in the evening when sunset colors gild its granite shaft. It is called Pilot Knob (12,227) and although sheer to the west, can be easily climbed from the east, and is an excellent point from which to survey the surrounding higher mountains, especially Mt. Humphreys, towering to the east across an undulating timberless basin.

One of the most beautiful of the lakes to the east of the Sierra crest is Convict Lake. On three sides of it rise picturesque mountains, the most imposing of which is Mt. Morrison, whose bold, sheer summit, 12,245 feet in elevation, rises to the south of the lake. Although obviously unscalable from the east, it probably can be ascended from the opposite direction. Along with most of the peaks of this group, it is remarkable for its richness of coloring — the red of the slate predominating amid the gray of quartzite and the black of schist.

A FEW miles to the west is Red and White Mountain, reported to be rather difficult of ascent. The majority found in this area are easy to climb, except that sometimes one encounters wearisome slopes of disintegrated slate. They form the northern terminus of the Southern Sierra. From them one looks northward and northwestward to the dark cluster consisting of Mts. Ritter, Banner and the Minarets; to the snowy summits of the Lyell group and the undulating skyline of those to the south and east of the headwaters of the Merced River.

The above sketchings may give those unacquainted with the Sierra Nevada some slight idea of the beauty and grandeur of the highest peaks in this lofty and magnificent range. However, it is only by climbing them that one can acquire a full appreciation of them. Even repeated ascents continually reveal something new, as no mountains are altogether the same on any two occasions. Of all the ranges in the United States there is probably none that offers such opportunity for strenuous but healthful mountain climbing as does the Sierra Nevada.

Mts. Lyell & McClure

Peaks of the Yosemite Region

ALTHOUGH NEITHER so high, so rugged nor so picturesque as the mountains of the southern Sierra, those of the Yosemite possess fascinating scenery and a considerable number of peaks sufficiently difficult to attract the attention of the climber.

As one looks northward from almost any of the loftier eminences of the southern Sierra his attention is always focused for a time on a dark, striking group consisting of Mts. Ritter, Banner and the Minarets situated between the headwaters of the north and the middle forks of the San Joaquin River, just outside of the boundary of the Yosemite National Park.

With the possible exception of the Mt. Lyell group they are the most impressive group of the region and are undoubtedly the most ruggedly Alpine. Forming a somewhat isolated group, they are readily distinguished for great distances from several directions, especially from the axis of the Sierra and from the crest of the desert ranges to the east, while from a large portion of Mono County they are conspicuous as they rise in a spectacular fashion beyond the forested area of the Mammoth Lake region.

Mt. Ritter attains an elevation of 13,156 feet above sea-level, is the highest mountain north of the southern Sierra in the Sierra Nevada proper, and is generally regarded as the most difficult

TOURING TOPICS. August 1928

of the loftier mountains of the Yosemite region, and as one possessing one of the finest views in this part of the range. While not an unusually difficult mountain, it requires caution on the part of the amateur and even experienced mountaineers have at times failed to reach its summit. Although it has been climbed from the east, the routes usually followed are from the west and the north. There seems, however, to be some difficulty in following the former, as several parties have unwittingly gotten off it and missed their objective. Nor is it the most accessible side of the mountain. The best route appears to be one up the north face of the peak, that can be approached from either the northwest or the northeast by swinging around the west or the east shoulder of Mt. Banner just north of Mt. Ritter.

Arriving on the saddle between the two mountains, one follows a broad chute midway up the steep face to a point several hundred feet below the summit, where he swings to the left up a narrow shelf that reaches the crest about fifty yards east of the summit, to which he can easily walk. During summers having an unusual amount of snow some difficulty might be in this route. The panorama seen from the summit extends far over the desert mountains and valleys to the east. The immediate surroundings are extremely Alpine, being composed of craggy mountains and deep gorges.

RUNNING south from Mt. Ritter is a long line of dark pinnacles called the Minarets. The highest* of these has been scaled but once and is considered one of the most difficult rockclimbs of the Sierra. To the north of Mt. Ritter — so close as to be a twin peak — is Mt. Banner, a peak with a precipitous northern slope, but a gentle and easily scaled southern one. It stands out in a very spectacular fashion from Garnet and Thousand Island lakes. The latter is an ultramarine tarn lying in the shadow of the jagged Minarets. Handsome mountain hemlocks dot the northern slopes, while from the south and the west great chunks of snow and ice drop into its deep blue water where they float for days before they eventually melt. Other nearby interesting phenomena are the Devil's Postpile, a striking mass of basaltic columns a few miles to the east. and Rainbow Falls, a snow-

*Clyde Minaret

Norman Clyde on Tower Pk., 1940.
Photo by Parker Severson

44

white cataract plunging over dark lava rock, several miles to the south.

LOOKING northwestward from the summit of Mt. Ritter one sees a group of mountains of which the highest is Mt. Lyell (13,090'). It possesses the largest glacier in the Sierra Nevada and is undoubtedly the most beautiful mountain in the Yosemite region. In composition and prespective, as one views its glacier-mantled north flank rising abruptly at the head of Lyell Creek, it has appealed to many artists. The ascent is usually effected from the north across the glacier and up a chimney or over a rocky comb to the dark, granite summit that projects above the glacier. It is usually of only ordinary difficulty except late in the season, the glacier is sometimes covered with snow hummocks several feet in height that render progress difficult.

The view from the top is one of the finest in this part of the range. To the southeast it commands the Ritter group; to the south it looks down upon the upper cirque and canyon and across them to the Merced peaks and far beyond them to the massed peaks of the southern Sierra; to the north and the northwest, down into the wide Alpine basin of Tuolumne Meadow and across it to Mt. Conness and a score of rugged peaks in the northwestern portion of the park. Mt. McClure, to the west of Mt. Lyell can readily be climbed from the saddle between the two mountains. To the east of Mt. Lyell, across the Merced cirque is Mt. Rodgers, another 13,000-foot-peak worthy of an ascent.

From the top of Mt. Lyell, in a northeasterly direction one sees a group of mountains, differing from the usual sharply-cut granite peaks typical of the Sierra, in their rounded outlines and warmer colors, various hues of red, touched with a shade of light green from lichens and mineral stain. The most outstanding of these is Mt. Dana (13,050'). It can readily be climbed from the vicinity of Tioga Pass, the ascent being little more than a trudge up a steep slope of slate occurring in low shelves, angular rocks, and toward the summit, of loose scree. It overlooks the steep eastern scarp of the Sierra — here about 7500 feet — across the circular, gray-green expanse of Mono Lake, eastward over range after range of desert mountains; southward past the Ritter group to the southern Sierra; northwestward along the ragged peaks along the northern border of the park.

Being at the head of Tuolumne Meadow it possesses a very fine prospect down this oval basin some ten miles in length, the Tuolumne River winding sinuously through verdant meadows that rise gently to deep green belts of conifer forest which sweep up to the gray snow-splashed peaks forming the skyline on either side of it.

SOMEWHAT more than half way down the meadow and to the south of it is a cluster of unusually sharp peaks that shoot up abruptly from pineclad slopes. They rise in isolated spires and ragged ridges that have been termed "cockcombs". The best known of these are the Unicorn and Cathedral peaks. Both are somewhat difficult ascents, the former demanding some rather delicate rock-work along a broken knife-edge, to reach the summit, a narrow rock 10,849 feet above sea-level. The latter involves a steep scramble that terminates in a twenty-foot climb up a vertical monolith that rises from a shelving alcove which pitches over a precipice. Two parallel cracks, several feet apart, extend up its face and into these the climber thrusts hands and feet, working up to the summit, a platform a few feet in diameter and 10,933 feet above sea-level. Persons wearing rubber-soled shoes may spiral around the final rock in a slightly different course. Both have excellent views of the northern half of the park.

North of the lower portion of Tuolumne Meadow is a handsome, light gray mountain that from many points to the south stands in fine perspective at the head of receding canyons. This is Mt. Conness (12,556'). The ascent is comparatively easy, varied by several hundred feet of steep climbing just below the summit, which drops away in vertical crags to the southwest and breaks rapidly down to a small glacier on the north. It commands an extensive view, especially of the series of rough peaks that run westward from it, forming the northern boundary of the park and a large area of the lower but interesting mountains to the

47

north of the park.

If one continues on the trail north of the Tuolumne River that in
a distance of eighteen miles leaps in snowy cascades and whirl-
ing water-wheel falls until it is eventually ensconced in a great
canyon with walls a mile high, he will cross a number of canyons which he can follow up to their heads at the base of the
peaks along the northern boundary of the park to Dunderberg
Peak, a dark slate mountain with a good view, or he can wind
up Matterhorn Canyon through groves of exquisite mountain
hemlocks — where insects have not killed them — to the Matterhorn that offers an excellent but not very difficult rock-climb to
its narrow summit that overlooks a fine panorama extending far
along the axis of the range — south to the southern Sierra, north
over undulating mountains that rise again in the mountains a-
round Lake Tahoe. Directly to the west of the Matterhorn is a
fine line of granite sawtooths. Along the main trail, a few miles
farther west, around Rodgers Lake, an extremely beautiful lake
are several peaks that are worthy of a scramble to their summits while along the northwestern limit of of the park is Tower Peak (11,702'), a rather isolated mountain that affords both
a good climb and an extensive view.

RETURNING to the lower portion of Tuolumne Meadow and
looking southwest one sees Mt. Hoffman, an apparently flat-
topped mountain not of great height but situated in a central and
somewhat isolated position that causes it to command one of the
best views to be had of Yosemite Park in its length and breadth.
It was one of the favorite mountains of John Muir. The ascent
can be easily made from the Tioga Road that passes several
miles to the south. Just north of the peak is Nine Lake Basin,
containing a considerable number of beautiful tarns counter-sunk
as it were, in a rocky terrain and overhung by groves of grace-
ful mountain hemlocks. Nearby them to the north are several
points from which one looks down into the Grand Canyon of the
Tuolumne River.

As one looks eastward from almost any of the numerous vantage
points that rise on either side of the Yosemite Valley, he is im-

pressed by a number of fine peaks that shut in the upper Merced Valley to the south. Striking in summer, they are more so in winter when their craggy peaks rise from undulating plateaus and deep basins covered by a stainless robe of snow. The most imposing of these is Mt. Clark. Its bold, sharp peak, of the Matterhorn type, rises so abruptly as to render it much more spectacular than would be expected from its actual height, which is only 11,506 feet. Although it can be climbed up the steeply shelving western face, the usual route followed is from the north which is an easy one except for a few rods of rather eerie knife-edge just below the top which is only a few feet in diameter. This peak, whose rock structure indicates that it was orginally a dome, has been attacked on three sides by glaciers that have carved it into a typical Matterhorn with three arêtes running out from a narrow summit. It is the best example of this type of mountain to be found in the Yosemite. The panorama seen is especially fine, extending to the distant south along the higher portion of the Sierra that rises majestically in the distance across a great depression.

RUNNING eastward from Mt. Clark are Gray, Merced and Triple Divide peaks, all readily scalable from the upper Merced. The views from all are excellent, that from Triple Divide Peak being perhaps the most noteworthy, as it stands between the watersheds of the Merced, both the main and the south forks, and a tributary of the San Joaquin. It is a slate mountain as are also one or two of its neighbors to the west. Mt. Florence to the east of Merced Lake can be climbed from it as a starting point. The upper Merced Canyon and amphitheatre is an interesting region. In addition to its beautiful mountains are the fine cascades and apron-falls of its higher reaches, and the emerald green Merced meandering through groves of tamarack pine and quaking aspen above Washburn Lake.

Although surpassed by the southern Sierra in loftiness and ruggedness, the Yosemite region is superior to it in waterfalls and cascades and in addition contains the Yosemite Valley. As a whole, although not as epic in grandeur as the southern portion of the range, it is a fascinating region with few equals.

50

Selected Writings of Clyde

These "Close Ups" of our High Sierra were only a small part of the material in TOURING TOPICS-WESTWAYS that Clyde contributed in the late twenties and early thirties. He also wrote for the journals of the various mountaineering clubs, for a few sporting magazines, and for the "sunday supplements" of several newspapers.

From these have been selected an account of the first ascent of the east face of Whitney, a recent article on avalanches, and the story of the first climb of Mt. Russell. Of the last, A CLIMBER'S GUIDE OF THE HIGH SIERRA says, "This peak presents a formidable appearance from almost every direction, and was one of the last of the major Sierran peaks to be climbed."

The First Ascent of Mount Russell

FOR SEVERAL days in the latter part of June, 1926, I was encamped in a grove of foxtail pines on a branch of Wallace Creek, formerly known as East Fork of Kern River. The location was a delightful one, commanding a fine outlook across the broad basin of the Kern to the lofty and picturesque Kaweahs, to the rugged array of peaks that form the Great Western Divide, and to a portion of the Kings-Kern Divide. The days were remarkably beautiful. The sky was usually clear in the morning, but each afternoon great masses of soft, fluffy cumulus clouds would gather about the western peaks. Presently they would float lazily across the blue sky to the peaks along the main crest of the Sierra, where they appeared to linger for a while before drifting eastward to vanish in the dry atmosphere above Owens Valley.

On the morning of the 24th of June I set out to climb Mount Russell (14,190 feet). Turning eastward, I gradually ascended the stream and passed through the upper glaciated basins until I reached Tulainyo Lake, at an elevation of 12,865 feet above sea level. This is unique in its location upon the very crest of the range, with no apparent outlet. It is almost circular in form, about half a mile in diameter, and possesses an air of remoteness and isolation not often encountered. Seldom has human foot trodden its almost vegetationless slopes from which rise abruptly several granite peaks, the highest of which is Mount Russell.

SIERRA CLUB BULLETIN, 1927

Mt. Russell
Photo by Norman Clyde.

53

I had given some consideration to the best method of approaching this mountain. During the previous autumn, from a nearby peak I had noted a narrow ridge, or knife-edge, leading upward toward the summit. Although it was too deeply gashed to permit one to follow its crest, there appeared to be a shelf on the northern side that might perhaps be used to a point not far below the summit. It was with this purpose of reaching this knife-edge that I was making a half-circuit to the east of the peak.

AFTER luncheon I continued southward over patches of deep snow and across a stretch of rough talus to the base of a ridge which, being only about five hundred feet in height, was soon surmounted. The route ahead looked formidable — at times impossible. To the south the wall dropped abruptly; to the north after descending at a steep angle for a few feet, it fell away sheer. Difficult as it seemed from a distance, nevertheless the way opened up as I progressed. There was always a safe passage and there were always enough protuberances and crevices to afford secure handholds and footholds. Now and then I came to a gash in the ridge through which I looked with a thrill down vertical cliffs, hundreds of feet in height, to the basin below.

After reaching the end of the ledge, a short scramble brought me to the eastern summit of the mountain. Thence a knife-edge extends a few hundred yards to the western peak, which is apparently the higher. The whole summit, in fact, is nothing more than a knife-edge with a high point at either end. Picking my way along the crest or along shelves a short distance below it, I advanced toward the western eminance, which I reached by hoisting myself over some large granite blocks. There was no cairn or other evidence of a previous ascent.

It was just such an eyrie as delights the heart of a mountaineer. Only a few feet in diameter, the summit drops away vertically to the south and the west and at a very steep angle to the north. The view was superb. To the south across a narrow cirque rose the precipitous eastern front and northern flank of Mount Whitney, seen from this point in its imposing aspect. Beyond, to the southeast, was an array of craggy mountains, and westward across the wide basin of the Kern were the stately and imposing Kaweahs and the ragged line of peaks of the Great Western Divide. To the north the eye followed the crest of the Sierra as far as the Palisades, with Goddard, Darwin and Humphreys looming hazy in the distance.

A S I SAT on the rocky summit in the warm sunshine, the radiant white clouds that lazily passed overhead gradually became denser and assumed a darker hue. Clouds were gathering in threatening masses around the Kaweahs and the Great Western Divide and seemed to be moving in mass upon a peak west of Mount Russell. Mindful of previous unpleasant encounters with electric storms on mountain-tops, I considered it time to seek lower elevations. Returning to the eastern summit I paused, debating whether I should follow the route used in the ascent or attempt a descent down an arete to the north. I decided upon the latter course, although it might entail a return to the summit. There was still a good deal of snow on the north face; to avoid the shelving glaciated slopes that cover a good portion of that side of the mountain, I followed the crest of the knife-edge or made my way along shelves immediately to the west of it. In the meantime the storm passed harmlessly by.

On the whole, less difficulty was encountered in the descent than I had anticipated. The joint-planes of the rock were rather far apart, and it was sometimes necessary to make a rather long drop in getting down from some hugh block. Eventually a rather formidable wall appeared to bar farther progress. On one side was a vertical clif, on the other a steeply shelving slope; but by an assortment of gymnastic maneuvers familiar to every rock-climber I was able to let myself down in safety to the base of this obstacle. Thence I sped down a snow-slope, hurried onward along a stream, past a lake, and safely reached my camp in the grove of foxtail pines near the base of Mount Barnard.

Up the East Face of Mt. Whitney

A MONG MOUNTAINEERS, second in fascination to the making
of first ascents is the finding of new routes up mountains already climbed, especially if these be difficult. As opportunities
of accomplishing the former gradually diminish, climbers turn
their attention to the discovery of new and more arduous ways
of obtaining the summits of mountains. Walking or riding being
a rather tame mode of reaching them, in their estimation, they
are forever seeking new problems of ascent against which they
may match their skill and strength, puny as these may be, compared with the forces of lofty mountains.

Scalable with comparative ease from the south, west and north,
Mt. Whitney, the highest peak in the United States, has lured
mountaineers in quest of a "real climb." Last season a fairly
difficult one was found going from the east up a broad chute culminating in a notch on an arete running northward from the peak,
and giving access to the north face which was followed to the summit. Unsatisfied with the discovery, however they began to consider whether the apparently sheer east face of Mt. Whitney
might not be scaled.

It was with this object in view that a party of five motored westward from Lone Pine toward the base of the Sierra Nevada during the forenoon of August 15 of the present year. The group
was one of proven climbing ability. It consisted of Dr. Under-

TOURING TOPICS, December 1931

East Face of Mt. Whitney
Offical U.S. Navy photograph.

hill of Harvard University, one of the most expert rockclimbers in the United States; Francis Farquhar of San Francisco, prominent in the activities of the Sierra Club; Jules Eichorn from the same city and Glen Dawson from Los Angeles, both youths, but very skillful in rockclimbing; and the writer of this sketch. It is pertinent too, that the first descent of the new route was made by three Los Angeles youths: Walter Brem, Richard Jones and Glen Dawson, on September 6, 1931.

Having arrived at the end of the road, some eight miles west of Lone Pine, we transferred our baggage from automobiles to the backs of several mules. After a short trudge up the sun-steeped eastern slope of the range we swung around a shoulder and entered the refreshing coolness and shade of Lone Pine Canyon with the summit of Mt. Whitney looking down from its head a few miles directly to the west. Charmed by the alluring seclusion of the gorge with floor shaded by pine and fir; with brook resounding through a canopy of birch and willow, with walls of mellow-hued and pleasingly-sculptured granite, we leisurely followed the trail to Hunter's Flat, a distance of about four miles, and continued up the switchbacks to the south of it to an elevation of some 9,000 feet above sealevel. There the packs were removed from the mules.

A FTER eating luncheon we fitted our packs on our backs and, abandoning the trail, began to pick our way up the North Fork of Lone Pine Creek. Within a few hundred feet we came upon a projecting buttress around which we swung, and began to scramble over broken rocks in the direction of a crevice leading up a steeply-shelving granite slope to a ledge running along the south wall of the gorge. Occasionally we stopped to regale ourselves in the luscious wild currants which grew abundantly among the chaotic talus through which we were passing. Below us the stream bounded along sonorously, hidden from view by a dense growth of birch and maple.

Upon arriving at the foot of the crevice, we scrambled up it as best we could, laden with heavy and bulky packs, to a ledge which we followed around a projection. Although the ledge

58

shelved down to a cliff, we strode rapidly along it in our rubber soled shoes, pausing now and then to look down to the floor of the canyon several hundred feet below us, or turning about to gaze eastward through its U-shaped opening and across the wide basin of Owens Valley to the Inyo Mountains — richly-colored, glowing in the afternoon sunshine, and with a mass of snowy-white cumulus clouds hovering above them. A scattering of limber pines grew along the lower portion of the shelf and as it gradually ascended, considerable numbers of the foxtail variety began to appear. To our left a vertical wall of granite rose in places to a height of several hundred feet.

HAVING reached the upper end of the shelf, we crossed a strip of talus to the border of a glacially-formed basin in which grew a beautiful grove of foxtail pines. Through these we filed along to the margin of a meadow at an altitude of some 10,000 feet. It was a fascinating spot, by craggy peaks and to the west of the great pinnacles and steep walls of Mt. Whitney. Being without a trail and difficult of access, seldom has human foot trodden its secluded recess, although but a few miles from Owens Valley. Presently the sun sank behind the serrated peaks of Mt. Whitney suffusing a few clouds that wreathed about their summits, with vivid-hued light.

The ensuing dawn was literally "rosy-fingered," the peaks of Mt. Whitney and those on either side of the cirques glowing in roseate light of marvelous beauty. After a hasty breakfast, we were soon on our way northward across the meadow, hoary with frost, to the base of a slope which we ascended to a cleft in the rock up which we scrambled to an apron-like slope of glaciated granite. Across this we picked our way along a series of cracks to a grove of foxtail pine in another basin.

With this behind us, we clambered up the point of a long promontory extending eastward from a shallow basin directly to the east of Mt. Whitney. Along its narrow crest we sped nimbly to the margin of the upper basin when we halted for a few minutes in order to survey the face of Mt. Whitney, but being able to make little of it, we walked northwestward a few hundred feet to a small lake which afforded a more satisfactory view. After careful scrutiny, a possible route was discovered. At best, however, it would obviously be a difficult one and any one of a number of apparent "gaps" in it might render it impracticable.

UP A STEEP acclivity sufficiently broken to permit easy progress we steadily climbed to the notch and there roped up. Dr. Underhill and Glen Dawson were on one rope; Jules Eichorn and myself on the other. The first rope proceeded along the shelf, but as feared, it suddenly terminated in a sheer wall. Upon hearing this, the second rope began to scale the face of the gendarme, but this proving rather hazardous, we swung to the right and succeeded in finding a narrow shelf, or rather the edge of an upright rock slab with a crevice behind it, along which we made our way to a notch beyond the pinnacle. From this we descended a few feet, rounded a protruding buttress on narrow ledges, and began to ascent a chute, rather steep but with surface sufficiently roughened to afford good footing.

After an ascent of a few hundred feet we entered an alcove-like recess where further direct advance was barred by a perpendicular wall. There we awaited rope number one which presently arrived and after a short pause climbed over a low ridge into another chimney, rope number two following. Both ropes then clambered up an overhang to a platform. From this, however, progress upward could be made only by climbing a steep and rather precarious crack. Rather than run the risk of a fall we decided to attempt a traverse around a buttress to the left to a slabby chimney beyond it.

As I swung out over the wall below the platform, an apparently firm rock gave way beneath my foot and went crashing down the sheer cliffs directly below, but as no one was in its path and my handholds were good, no harm resulted.

Rope number one then went around the buttress to reconnoiter and after a pause of some time the other followed. The traverse proved to be one requiring considerable steadiness, as these ledges were narrow and there was a thousand feet of nothing below them. As we came around the projection we were confronted by a gap in a ledge with a narrow platform about eight feet below. There was the alternative of stepping across it — as far as a man of medium height could possibly reach, availing himself of rather poor handholds — or dropping down to the platform and climbing the other side of the gap. Some of the members of the party chose one method; some the other.

Once over the break in the ledge we were obliged to pull ourselves over a rounded rock by clinging to a diagonal crack with our hands while our feet momentarily swung out over the thousand-foot precipice. We then attacked a precipitous slabby wall availing ourselves of narrow ledges for hand and footholds. A few rods of this, however, brought us to a rounded shoulder with a broad couloir above it.

AFTER halting a short time for luncheon we proceeded up the chimney, zigzagging back and forth as we clambered over and around great granite steps until we were confronted at the upper end of the chimney by a vertical wall about thirty feet in height. At one side of it, however, there was a narrow crevice up which one might scramble. After removing our rucksacks, we squirmed and corkscrewed up it, the last man tying the knapsacks to the rope carried by the first.

Above the couloir, somewhat to our surprise, we encountered rather easy climbing. We therefore unroped and began to as - cend to the right toward the summit of Mt. Whitney. Within a few minutes we came within sight of a cairn a little more than two hundred feet above us.

QUICKENING our speed, we clambered hastily upward, arriving at the summit, considerably elated by the successful accomplishment of the first ascent of Mt. Whitney up its apparently unscalable eastern face. Francis Farquhar, having ascended the mountain by another route, was there to meet us.

After spending an hour or more on the top of Mt. Whitney, the party separated, three following the trail southward in order to ascend Mt. Muir, while Dr. Underhill and myself proceeded to descend the north face to a notch a few hundred feet below the summit. It was an easy descent along a rocky rib and down a wide chute to the right of it.

After an evening spent in consuming enormous quantities of food and lounging about a campfire, we retired to our sleeping bags under nearby foxtail pines solemnly silent beneath a sky spangled with innumerable stars over-arching the mountains that loomed darkly around the basin. On the following morning we made up our packs and proceeded down the canyon, pleased at having added another outstanding climb to the already discovered number in the Sierra Nevada.

High Sierra Avalanches

A VALANCHES ARE much more numerous in the High Sierra during the winter and spring than those who have not spent considerable time there are aware. Their number varies greatly being much more frequent and of greater volume during seasons of high precipitation. That comparatively slight damage has been done to property and few lives lost is due, in large measure, to the fact that most occur when there is little property to destroy and no person in the pathway.

With the annual increase of visitors to the Sierra for skiing and climbing, the hazard to life and limb is enhanced, particularly to those who do not know when or where slides may occur. Those who do may not come to grief in a single season.

Snowslides in the higher portions of the mountains take place most frequently in couloirs or chutes. After heavy snowfalls, numerous slides course down. They are most likely in winter or within the day following a storm. In spring, after a storm, almost as soon as the sunshine strikes new snow, it may let go and come rushing down the couloir. After a storm in May, I have seen as many as a dozen slides coursing down as many couloirs in beautiful snowfalls.

Avalanches take place on smooth slopes on steep mountain faces. Powder snow does not cling to these faces. If it happens to be wet, as sometimes happens, even in the High Sierra, a considerable amount may adhere to the rocks. As the temperature warms this usually sloughs off in avalanches.

During winters of heavy snowfall, slides may occur in unexpected places. They may even come down rough south-facing slopes where slides seldom or never take place during winters of normal snowfall. Snowslides may sweep all the snow down to the underlying rocks, perhaps taking along the rocks. Then the avalanche gives a crashing sound as it goes plunging down. If composed almost entirely of snow, it may only give a hissing sound, audible for no great distance. If of powder snow and the volume is great, a cloud of flying snow will be carried high into the air.

MANY slides do not reach the underlying terrain. Except on protected slopes or basins, snow that falls in the Sierra may be packed by the wind or thaw on the surface. As the temperature drops, a crust is formed. If alternate thawing and freezing continues, nevé, or granular snow is formed, By spring, much of the snow, particularly on exposed slopes is of this form.

Rough slopes which would prevent snow from sliding are sometimes smoothed over. Should a heavy snow fall on such a surface, particularly if the slope is above 45°, the danger of a slide is great. Many of the spring slides are of this type. Often these are not dangerous unless one happens to be in a confined space, such as a couloir, or if they happen to be a sheet-slide so wide that one cannot get beyond their margin.

Slides in the Sierra are likely to be narrow. After a storm, I have seen numerous ones of new snow come down, each making a peculiar hissing sound. I have skied across the path of one and, wheeling, watched the slide sweep with its peculiar sliding rolling motion. Avalanches usually start slowly. A crack runs along, then slowly widens and a sheet of snow begins to move. Once started, the acceleration may be great. If it travels three thousand feet down a steep slope, it may reach express-train speed. Its momentum being sufficient, it may run across sev-

Mt. Tom
Photo by Norman Clyde

64

eral hundred yards of terrain at the foot. If the slide results from a collapsing cornice, it may, however, simply go plunging down the mountainside.

GENERALLY, there is little danger to one who knows when and where snowslides may occur. In many years of rambling about at high elevations, only on two occasions did I incur any such danger. Once, after climbing through a notch on the upper rim of a cliff and entering a couloir, I stepped to one side. As I did so, I heard a swishing sound, and an avalanche swept down the notch through which I had just climbed.

On another occasion, weary of slogging through wet snow well up to my knees, I hit upon the idea of starting miniature snow-slides and riding them. This I did by sitting down heavily, causing the layer of new snow to begin to slide. The acceleration was rapid. Eventually I struck a shadowed area, where an icy crust had formed.

Instantly, the slide shot forward, with a cliff only a short distance ahead. By swimming and rolling, I managed to get off the slide and watched it vanish over the cliff.

That was the last time that I deliberately rode a snowslide.

Mt. Ritter & Banner Pk. R. D.

A Half Century of Climbing

1914 WAS the first year that I did any climbing of any account in the Sierra. Climbing at that time was what mountaineers sometimes term "free climbing." Ropes were seldom used and those that were, were not adequate and probably no one knew anything about the technique of using a rope in climbing. An ice axe was seldom or never seen. Any ice cutting that was done was usually done with some sort of a wood axe. As to foot gear, there was a tendency to wear at least moderately high boots. These were often of a very good grade and their owner was oft-times quite proud of them. Often they were provided with Hungarian nails or hobnails. The former were fairly satisfactory until worn flat, so that the wearer was likely to do considerable skating around on smooth rocks.

In the twenties there was considerable change. Personally, I learned the technique of rope climbing from Swiss guides and the Canadian Alpine Club in the Canadian Rockies. Thereafter, I seldom did any serious climbing without carrying a standard seven-sixteenth-inch rope or a lighter one, which I called an "emergency" rope and which was adequate for roping down; what was coming to be known as rappelling and for occasional belaying. Ice axes were seen occasionally. A few climbers took to wearing boots provided with Swiss edge nails. Somewhat later I changed to Tricouni nails. These were better on snow and ice than the edge nails, but not too satisfactory on smooth hard rock. For rock climbing, I usually carried a pair of rubber-soled shoes — preferably crepe rubber — in my rucksack. Most Sierra climbers had some sort of rubber-soled shoes in reserve.

The techniques of rope climbing gradually improved, also "hardware" climbing came more or less in vogue, particularly on the walls of Yosemite. At first pitons were used merely as a safety precaution reserve on difficult pitches. Some climbers, however, came to depend more and more upon them, and were able to make climbs that otherwise would be impossible.

LATER, in the matter of footgear, there was a gradual change from nailed soles to cleated rubber ones, at first to the Bramani design. Somewhat later a further change was made to the Vibram type, which came near to being an all-around satisfactory mountain climbing boot than any other boot yet produced. Climbers, who encountered much ice and snow may supplement these with crampons.

Today, climbers in the High Sierra may be roughly divided into several groups. One group, which may be the walkers, seldom goes past Class 2 climbing. These often do not carry rope. Another group is satisfied with Class 3 and Class 4 grades, seldom going beyond. These usually do and always should carry a rope and often carry along a few pitons and carabiners, to help themselves over a difficult pitch. If there is snow and ice, they add an ice axe. Lastly, are the technical rock climbers, who are not happy unless they encounter a liberal measure of Class 5 and Class 6 pitches.

All forms are legitimate, if proper safety measures are followed. There is room for all. Some may not think "hardware climbing" is justified on account of the supposed risks involved. Properly equipped and careful climbers, however incur less dangerous exposure on Class 5 and Class 6 routes than untrained men inadvertently may on Class 3, or even Class 2. Everyone to his taste. "De gustibus non disputandum est," as the old Latin proverb goes.

Baker Ranch, 1961   Norman Clyde

Norman Clyde

Norman Clyde

NORMAN CLYDE, a name as legendary as that of Fremont or Muir. Norman Clyde, a man to whom the entire High Sierra was as familiar as one's own back yard. Norman Clyde, whose own life is much less known than that of the Greek heroes whose sagas he packed in his rucksack.

And how did this come about? For Norman was a quiet, often taciturn man. He had often failed to leave a record of his achievements, had never been heard to boast of his fabulous ascents. Yet, since he made his first trip to the top of Mt. Whitney, over sixty long years ago, climbers have been finding his records on remote summits. A strong team of skilled rockclimbers will conquer a lonely spire, using the most modern of climbing gear and techniques and win through with well co-ordinated teamwork to find on a faded Kodax box the record of a solo climb of many decades ago. Or, at the high point of a distant ridge will be found a small cairn, but no written record. Obviously the work of man, and one mountaineer will turn to his companion with, "Well, it sure looks like a first ascent, except for Norman Clyde." Later, discussing the route with him, Clyde would ponder a bit; asked a couple of questions about some difficult pitch encountered on the ascent, then admit he had been there—a score or more years ago.

Clyde had never been one to bring up these mountaineering achievements; would often sidestep them, or give a facitious answer, such as saying that he was "350 years old", but never had Clyde been known to make a false statement when talking seriously. And it was easy to tell the difference between his banter and his true accounts of his life and his work. Research uniformly verifies the date and data that he had supplied.

Norman's father, Charles Clyde was born in Antrim County in the north of Ireland in 1854. He migrated to this country at the age of seven. His mother, born Belle (Isabel) Purvis, was a native of Butler, a small city about thirty miles north of Pittsburg. Charles and Belle were married at Butler and took up residence in Philadelphia, where Norman Asa, the first of nine children, was born the following year, on April 8, 1885. His father was a self-taught clergyman of the Covenanter sect of the Presbyterian faith.

WHEN Norman was three, the family moved to Ohio. Here, his father served at a number of small churches, seldom staying more than a year at any one parsonage. Apparently the independence of thought that was later to dictate Norman's flight to the mountains was honestly inherited. Eventually, the family moved to Glengarry County, near Ottawa. Norman remembers arriving there on the Queen's Jubilee Day (May 24, 1897).

Here Norman lived from the time he was twelve until he was seventeen. Fishing and hunting were available, almost in the Clyde's backyard, and he soon became expert in both. Clyde's father, being self-taught, took care of his son's schooling at home. His father was an avid student of the classics and the boy was learning to read Latin and Greek almost as early as he did his native tongue.

His father was stricken with pneumonia and passed away at the age of 46. His mother gathered up her flock and returned to western Pennsylvania. Norman enrolled in Geneva College at Beaver Falls, but as he had had no formal schooling, he had several deficiencies to make up at the prep level. Graduating in the classics from Geneva in June, 1909 he immediately started west. He taught at several small rural schools across the country, including Fargo, North Dakota, and Mt. Pleasant, Utah. One summer was spent at the University of Wisconsin, John Muir's alma mater; another on a cattle spread in Utah.

Deciding that he needed more education to progress in the teaching field, he enrolled at the University of California at Berkeley in 1911. Summers were spent in the mountains and in teaching at summer schools. One was at Elko, Nevada, where he spent his spare time climbing in the Humboldt Range.

At the end of two years at the university, Clyde found that he still lacked one course in Romance Drama and his thesis. He balked at the drama course, maintaining that Italian plays should be read in Italian, French dramas in French; neither in English. He could see no sense in struggling with a thesis that nobody would ever read after he received his degree, so he quietly left the university without his master's degree.

DURING the next dozen years, the details of Clyde's life are rather sketchy, both in and out of the mountains. We learn that he taught in a number of small schools in central and northern California. He remembers teaching near Stockton and spent a year each at Mt. Shasta and Weaverville. From his mountaineering notes, he must have spent some time in Arizona. Sometime during this period he married a young lady from Pasadena. This is one part of his life that Norman refuses to discuss. It is known that they lived together for three years, and that she passed away from tuberculosis. It is apparent that he felt a deep love for his bride, and undoubtedly her passing was a strong factor in shaping his character.

In the field of mountaineering, we have a few more records. He was in Yosemite in 1914, where he first met up with the Sierra Club, joining with them on a trip to Tuolumne. Clyde became a member of the club that year. After leaving the club outing, he travelled south along the backbone of the Sierra with a packtrain run by Charley Robinson, oldtime Sierra packer. The trip ended at Lone Pine, and Clyde made the first of his fifty ascents of Mt. Whitney at this time. Records show twelve ascents of Mt.

Shasta, including three in four days. On one of these he set a record that only has been broken once since that time. Another page of his notes lists seven ascents of Weaver Bally in the Trinity country.

We know that Clyde accompanied the Sierra Club on their trip from Yosemite through Evolution Valley in 1920, during which time he made several first ascents. It was on this trip that he carried the first of his famous big packs. Leaving the Valley a couple of days behind the Sierra Club and not knowing for sure whether he could catch up with the club, he took along sufficient food. As he swung by Camp Curry, noticing a platform scale, he weighed the pack at seventy-five pounds. The next night was spent with a survey crew that he had met on the trail. They seemed amazed at the size of the pack (at that time Clyde weighed but 140 pounds) and kept commenting about it. In the morning, one of the crew suggested that Norman might have trouble finding the packtrain and suggested that he take along a few extra cans of food that they had. Another offered a couple of other items. As later companions were to find out, Norman never turns down free supplies, and the group kept offering him more, telling of the dangers of being caught in the wilderness without food. After they had loaded him down with an additional twenty pounds, he was allowed to go his way. It was not until the next day that Clyde realized it had all been a gag to see how much he could carry, but it is still a question as to which side came out ahead with the gag.

In the fall of 1924, Clyde was appointed principal of the high school at Independence in Owens Valley. Situated at the foot of Mt. Williamson, probably the most magnificent of all of the 14,000-footers, it was withing easy driving distance of most of the approaches to the High Sierra. Every weekend, he would lock up his school and dash off for the peaks. The record for 1925 shows that he logged 48 climbs, of which exactly half were first ascents. Only on six of the total number did he have a climbing companion. The following year, the number of ascents was boosted to sixty, that is sixty that have been recorded. Norman was exploring the range at a rate that far surpassed the records of Brewer, Clarence King or John Muir.

However a number of the townspeople were not so impressed by this record. Certainly Clyde was an excellent instructor and he controlled the wild youths of this mountain valley like they had never been controlled before. But a school teacher, especially a principal, was supposed to be an important man in the social and cultural life of the community. On Sunday, he should be attending one of the local churches. On Friday night, if there were a school social function, the principal was an honored, if captive, guest. Many of the neighbors were openly stating that Independence High needed a principal that would act as a principal should, rather than a crazy mountain climber.

Then came Halloween of 1927. Rumor had it that the boys were going to play many a prank on the school facilities and it seemed that these were not to be harmless pranks. Norman stationed himself nearby, armed with a .38-cal revolver. As a carload of youths drove onto the school grounds, he challenged them. They refused to stop, so he fired a warning shot. Apparently the rowdies belived that Clyde could be bluffed and kept on. He fired a second shot, which ricochetted fragments of lead onto the car. The hoodlums left and soon were telling the story all over the town, taking the whole thing as a huge joke.

NOT SO their parents — they waited upon the sheriff and demanded a warrant for attempted murder. The sheriff turned down this request, saying that if Clyde had attempted murder, it would have been murder, as he was the best pistol shot in the county. Next a request was made for a complaint charging illegal use of firearms. After a few days, Clyde resigned; all charges were dropped and Independence had traded its most colorful principal for a teacher that would act as a teacher should act.

No longer tied to regular amployment, he plunged into a fulltime study of the High Sierra. Within the next year a large number of articles poured from his pen, including the well-known series "Close Ups" of our High Sierra that appeared in Touring Topics (now Westways) in the spring and summer of 1928.

Summers were spent in climbing in the back country. At times

Clyde would guide parties to the summits of difficult peaks, and it made no difference if the climbers were a USGS party attempting to place a bench mark on an "unscalable" summit or a lady peak-bagger; they made their peaks with Norman Clyde.

Winters were usually spent serving as a caretaker at a mountain resort. Thus he was able to hole-in at such places as Glacier Point at Yosemite, Giant Forest at Sequioa, Parcher and Andrews camps on Bishop Creek, Glacier Lodge above Big Pine, and at Whitney Portal, Many were the times that Clyde rescued lost or snowbound climbers, or if not called in time, located their bodies. His locating of wrecked planes has been the subject of numerous magazine stories.

In 1939, his alma mater, Geneva College, awarded him a degree of Doctor of Science in appreciation of his mountain writings.

━━━━━━━━━━━

DURING his last years, Clyde lived most of the time at the old Baker Ranch on Baker Creek, near Big Pine, California. He had a primitive three-room ranch house, using kerosene lanterns and having running water because a stream flowed through the spring house. His home and adjoining arbor were covered with a canopy of grapevines and climbing roses.

For a number of years, Clyde would spend part of each summer at Sierra Club Base Camps, where he would entertain at campfires with tales of his earlier years — always being available to chat with those who wished to hear directly from him of the early days in the Range of Light.

Unfortunately, Clyde was found to be suffering from an enlarged heart, and as he grew older it became obvious that he would require more attention. So his last few years were spent in a rest home near Big Pine — until he set out for his final ascent on the 23rd day of December, 1972.

Walt Wheelock

Selected Writings of Clyde

Touring Topics

Westways

Sierra Club Bulletin

Southern Sierran

CLYDE'S FIRST ASCENTS IN THE SIERRA NEVADA

Peak	Date	Source
Electra Pk. (12,442)	1914	CG
Parker Pk. (12,537)	1914	CG
Mt. Huxley (13,117)	August 1920	CG
Dragon Pk. (12,995)	1920	CG
Triple Divide Pk. (11,561)	1920	CG
Peak 12,415	July 1922	CG
Peak 11,920+ *	8-9-22	CG
Diamond Pk. (13,126)	August 1922	CG
Mt. Lippencott (12,260)	1922	CG
Mt. McAdie-no.pk. (13,680)	1922	CG
Gray Kaweah (13,680)	1922	MR
Mt. Irvine (13,770)	June 1925	CG
Mt. Le Conte (13,960)	June 1925	CG
Mt. Mallory (13,850)	June 1925	CG
North Guard (13,327)	7-12-25	CG
Mt. Genevra (13,055)	7-15-25	CG
Mt. Jordon (13,344)	7-15-25	CG
The Hermit (12,360)	8-2-25	SCB
Emerald Pk. (12,543)	8-8-25	CG
Peak 11,778	8-8-25	CG
Mt. Agassiz (13,891)	8-30-25	CG
Giraud Pk. (12,585)	9-1-25	CG
Peak 12,861	11-22-25	CG
Mt. Carillon (13,552)	1925	CG
Mt. Lamarck (13,417)	1925	CG
Lone Pine Pk. (12,944)	1925	CG
Kearsarge Pk. (12,598)	1925	CG
Peak 12,000+	1925	CG
Peak 12,400+	1925	MR
Peak 12,720+	1925	CG
Peak 13,040	1925	CG
Peak 13,231	1925	MR
Peak 13,360	1925	MR
Peak 12,320	4-4-26	CG
Candlelight Pk. (	June 1926	SCB
Peak 13,840+	6-22-26	CG
Mt. Russell (14,086)	6-24-26	CG
Trojan Pk. (13,950)	6-26-26	CG
Point 13,920+	6-27-26	CG
Mt. Emerson (13,225)	7-3-26	CG
Mt. Goethe (13,200+)	7-5-26	SCB
Peak 13,112	7-7-26	SCB
West Spur Pk. (12,240+)	9-19-26	CG
Peak 12,225	9-19-26	CG
Laurel Mtn. (11,812)	9-25-26	CG
Peak 13,165	11-14-26	CG
Independence Pk. (11,744)	1926	CG
Lookout Pt. (10,144)	1926	CG
Mt. Gayley (13,510)	6-10-27	CG
Inconsolable Range (13,501)	6-15-27	SCB
Deerhorn Mtn. (13,265)	7-8-27	CG
Piute Crags - No.5 (12,480+)	1927	CG
Peak 12,866	1927	CG
Mt. McAdie - middle pk. (13,680+)	June 1928	CG
Mt. Morrison (12,268)	6-22-28	CG
Clyde Minaret (12,281)	6-27-28	CG
Mt. Baldwin (12,614)	7-2-28	SCB
Bloody Mtn. (12,544)	7-3-28	CG
Mt. Gilbert (13,103)	9-15-28	CG
Mt. Rogers (12,800)	7-6-29	MR
Peak 13,917	6-9-30	CG
Peak 13,520+	6-14-30	CG
Peak 12,840+	7-4-30	CG
North Palisade - nw.pk. (14,160)	7-9-30	CG
Mt. Gilbert (13,103)	9-15-28	CG
Mt. Rogers (12,800)	7-6-29	MR
Peak 13,917	6-9-30	CG
Peak 13,520+	6-14-30	CG
Peak 12,840+	7-4-30	CG
North Palisade- nw.pk.(14,160)	7-9-30	CG
Basin Mtn. - w.pk. (13,240)	11-8-30	SCB
" " e.pk. (12,880+)	11-9-30	SCB
Peak 13,120+	6-27-31	CG
Peak 13,090	7-5-31	CG
Echo Peaks, No.3 (10,960+)	7-7-31	CG
Peak 13,355	7-16-31	SCB
Echo Peaks -highest (11,040+)	7-31-31	SCB
Thunderbolt Pk. (14,040)	8-13-31	CG
Peak 13,323	9-6-31	CG
Peak 12,571	9-29-31	CG
Table Mtn. (11,653)	10-24-31	CG
Peak 11,936	11-7-31	SCB
Four Gables (12,825)	1931	CG
Slide Mtn. (11,120+)	1931	CG
Pinnacle Ridge (13,040)	4-4-32	NC
Peak 12,640	5-26-32	NC
Peak 12,893	7-17-32	CG
Mt. Stewart (12,205)	8-14-32	CG
Mt. Hutchings (10,785)	1933	CG
Clyde Spires - n.pk'. (13,267)	7-22-33	CG
" " s.pk. (12,960+)	7-22-33	CG
Kehrlein Minaret (11,440+)	8-23-33	CG
Wotan's Throne (11,858)	1933	CG
Devil's Crags #10 (11,950)	6-23-34	CG
" " #11 (11,950)	6-23-34	CG
" " #3 (12,350)	6-24-34	CG
" " #4 (12,250)	6-25-34	CG
" " #5 (12,250)	6-25-34	CG
" " #6 (12,250)	6-25-34	CG
" " #7 (12,250)	6-25-34	CG
" " #8 (11,250)	6-25-34	CG
Mt. Morgan (13,005)	7-9-34	CG
Mt. Huntington (12,405)	7-14-34	CG
Peak 12,318	7-14-34	CG
Peak 12,408	7-16-34	MR
Mt. Hopkins (12,302)	7-16-34	CG
Peak 12,880+	7-18-34	CG
Peak 12,691	7-18-34	CG
Mono Rock (11,555)	7-18-34	CG
Peak 12,804	July 1935	CG
Peak 12,852	July 1935	CG
Peak 13,183	July 1935	CG
Peak 12,372	8-25-35	CG
Peak 12,400+	9-4-35	CG
Peak 13,045	9-14-35	CG
Peak 11,844	9-16-35	CG
Peak 11,719	9-16-35	CG
Peak 12,916	6-13-36	NC
Inconsolable Range (13,278)	6-15-37	CG
Mt. Izaak Walton (12,099)	7-20-38	NC
Peak 12,563	1938	CG
Goodale Mtn. (12,790)	7-23-39	CG
Kid Mtn. (11,896)	7-2-40	CG
Birch Mtn. (13,665)	?	CG)
Cardinal Mtn. (13,397)	'20s	SCB
Mt. Johnson (12,868)	before 1939	CG
Thor Pk. (12,300)	?	CG

CG = A Climber's Guide to the High Sierra, 1954
MR = Mountain Records of the Sierra Nevada, 1937

NC = Journals of Norman Clyde, unpublished.
*11,920+ = elevation of highest contour line.

INDEX